DEALING WITH DOUBLE-MINDEDNESS

Dealing with Double-Mindedness

WILLIAM E. HULME

1817

HARPER & ROW, PUBLISHERS, SAN FRANCISCO

Cambridge, Hagerstown, New York, Philadelphia
London, Mexico City, São Paulo, Sydney

DEALING WITH DOUBLE-MINDEDNESS. Copyright © 1982 by William E. Hulme. All rights reserved. Printed in the United States of America. No part of this book may be used or reproduced in any manner whatsoever without written permission except in the case of brief quotations embodied in critical articles and reviews. For information address Harper & Row, Publishers, Inc., 10 East 53rd Street, New York, NY 10022. Published simultaneously in Canada by Fitzhenry & Whiteside Limited, Toronto.

FIRST EDITION

Designer: Jim Mennick

Library of Congress Cataloging in Publication Data

Hulme, William Edward
    DEALING WITH DOUBLE-MINDEDNESS

    Includes bibliographical references.
    1. Decision (Christian theology) I. Title.
BT702.H84   1982   248.4'841   82-47745
ISBN 0-06-064079-0   AACR2

82 83 84 85 86 10 9 8 7 6 5 4 3 2 1

Contents

Preface

As I reflect on events in my life that I wish could have been different, I am sobered by the fact that more often than not I see my own double-mindedness contributing to those events. Some of them were only of incidental significance in the overall picture of my life, but some were important; consequently, I have more than an observer's interest in the ins and outs of double-mindedness.

The very word *double-mindedness* is a problem. Is it sufficiently clear in its meaning to be placed in a title, for example? Although everyone to whom I described double-mindedness understood it immediately, some were puzzled by the word before hearing the explanation. It is a "Berne-like" word originating in the New Testament letter of James.*

In the pages that follow, I describe how double-mindedness operates in our lives, as well as how we can deal with it. The choice of the word *deal* in conjunction with *double-mindedness* is both honest and realistic. We live within the confines of imperfection—it cannot once and for all be eradicated—yet there is much that we can do to curtail the destructive influence of double-mindedness.

After an initial chapter describing how double-mindedness may sabotage our efforts and weaken our assertion, I compare

---

* *Originating* is an apt description, since it appears that James may have actually coined the word. See *The Vocabulary of the New Testament* (London: Hodder & Stoughton, 1915), p. 166.

double-mindedness with self-doubt, as does James. Then I take up the causes of double-mindedness: fear and its antidote in trust, unresolved guilt and its resolution in reconciliation with who we are, and divided loyalty and its remedy in the hard but necessary choices we need to make—choices that determine our identity.

Problems in identity can be seen as problems of commitment, as I show in Chapter 6. We are torn between accepting our creaturely status as human beings and wanting instead to be like God. Knowing who is God helps us know who *isn't*—and thus helps us accept our creaturely limits. This focus on our limits contains the paradox discussed in Chapter 7: while on the one hand we resist our limits to satisfy our insatiable egos, we actually add to our limits for the protection of those same egos.

Double-mindedness has a good side as well: it counteracts simplistic assessments. One can be single-mindedly wrong or even evil. Chapter 8 suggests that the double-mindedness that comes from facing the complexity of any issue is a needed preliminary to good decisions.

Chapter 9 introduces the ultimate resolution to double-mindedness: our sense of calling. Purpose and meaning are tied up with the identity of one who is called by God to give and to receive and to enter again and again into the *new*.

Throughout these chapters I have used experiences from my counseling ministry as illustrations. The particulars in these incidents are changed to preserve the privacy of those involved.

Your Double-Mindedness
Will Trip You Up

During my first year in the ministry, I was asked by a former college friend to perform her marriage. She also asked that the ceremony take place in a specific restaurant. I wanted to say no—because I prefer to perform marriage ceremonies in the church—but I also wanted to please. So I said yes to her and no to myself. This is a classic example of double-mindedness. I got through the rehearsal all right, in spite of my double-mindedness and my discomfort with the setting. However, during the actual ceremony, as I pronounced them husband and wife, I said, "What God has put asunder, let not man join together." I realized immediately that I had reversed the words. I looked at the assembled people, and when they did not seem to register shock, I decided not to correct it. As I reflected on this "blooper" (hoping I had not put a curse on my friend's marriage), I realized that my double-mindedness had finally tripped me up.

Recently, I became aware of this same double-mindedness when on the way home from a week's vacation, my wife suggested we stop for supper. I said OK, but inwardly I thought we might just as well wait until we got home. But I said yes, and so we stopped. As we were looking at the menu, I could not see anything particularly attractive, and I felt my irritated no rising up to sabotage the event. But before I grumbled, "What did we come in here for?" or "Why didn't we keep driving until we got home?" I perceived the double-mindedness at work and decided not to let it trip me up. "Look, you're here now," I said to myself, "so make the most of the time. Affirm your yes!" As a result, we both enjoyed it. Had I not caught it—and it was close!—there would have been an unconscious attempt on my part to give my no its sabotaging opportunity. When in my vacillation I "say yes and no at once" (2 Cor. 1:17), I had better decide quickly which side to back! Otherwise the contradiction will cripple what efforts I make.

Major Obstacle to Growth

The double-mindedness that I see in myself I see also in many of the people whom I counsel. From my observation and experience, it is a major obstacle to growth and development. I take the term *double-mindedness* from Saint James, who uses it in his epistle to describe the blockage that prevents us from receiving what God wants to give. He encourages his readers to "ask in faith, with no doubting, for he who doubts is like a wave of the sea that is driven and tossed by the wind. For that person must not suppose that a double-minded man, unstable in all his ways, will receive anything from the Lord" (James 1:6–8).

James is an early analyst describing the complexities of the human psyche. Yet it would be a mistake to call him the Freud of the New Testament because of this. If that were the case, he would have labeled his observation of double-mindedness *ambivalence* (from the Latin) or some equivalent abstraction in Greek. In describing it instead as double-mindedness, he would better be called an early Eric Berne. Like transactional analyst Berne's terms, double-mindedness is from the vernacular and consequently easily understood. I use it often in pastoral counseling because of its clarity. People "get the point" with a minimum of explanation; "the light turns on" because it *fits*. The phenomenon it describes is frequently a factor in human problems.

The presence of double-mindedness throws a different light on the maxim Know your own mind. Knowing one's own mind may mean knowing one's own *double* mind. Life would be much simpler if we had a single mind and all we needed to do was affirm it. The same is true with the adage Be yourself. One would need to ask, "Which self?" This implies a choice—often a most difficult one. The process of self-affirmation is more complex than these simple aphorisms indicate. As our self-awareness expands, so also does the awareness of our options. The result is more freedom and with it more responsibility, since options call for choices. After I had confronted a counselee with my own insight in an attempt to expand his awareness, he responded, "One of my minds says that what you are saying is rubbish. The other says I had better listen. I think I'll decide for the latter."

Many of us project our double-mindedness onto external obstacles. It is then these obstacles that are preventing us from doing what we really would like to do. Should these obstacles be removed, we may "discover" the doubleness within. In problems of family life, for example, it may happen that even when the obstacles to change are removed, no change may occur. The problem then takes on an entirely different context. This was the case with John and Mary. John blamed his restlessness and apparent disinterest in his family on his job—it was not satisfying him. Mary, therefore, was willing to "pull up stakes" with their children and go with John to the university while he educated himself for another profession. John worked hard and did well, but Mary and the children saw even less of him than they did before. He had a study cubicle on campus because he said he could not concentrate on his studies in their student apartment. Mary was patient because John assured her that when he finished his schooling everything would be different.

But it was not. John threw himself into his new job with the same intensity he had his studies. Mary became frightened.

Was it never to be any different? In her fear, she began to complain, or in John's words, "nag." Probably because she was finally confronting him with the reality of his own double-mindedness, John lashed back at her. Soon their life was growing bitter with quarreling. Meanwhile, John was finding himself increasingly attracted to a woman with whom he worked. He justified his involvement by blaming Mary for the "nagging." The marriage ended soon after in divorce, and John was "spared" the reality of facing his own double-mindedness about being a husband to Mary and a father to their children.

Ironically, this same double-mindedness may be revealed when the so-called cause of family stress is removed. We cannot be sure, for example, that Mary would have responded positively to John even if things had been different after the deprivation in her life as a student's wife had ended. Sometimes families *need* one of their members to be a "problem." Although they may complain as well as worry about this member, they may not be pleased if this person changes. In fact, they may resist the change. Because of this possibility, family counselors Carl Whitaker and Augustus Napier strongly advise families to enter therapy together rather than just arranging therapy for the one with the "problem." "If you decide to enter therapy individually," they say, "you can be assured that if you begin to change, your family will be both upset and disheartened."[1] Why should those who want one to change resist such a change? Because it upsets the tenuous balance they have worked out concerning the source of their tension. Once they have located this source outside of themselves, they are double-minded about resolving it. Subconsciously they fear that there is more to their tension than this external source, and this "more" may be within them— something therefore less tangible, less manageable. They may not want to face this.

Bob was a professional person who was eager to succeed in his work. He often brought work home with him because he could not finish all that he wanted to do in his office. He also had a marital problem: his wife, he said, was frigid. Jane acknowledged that she was unresponsive but insisted that she was turned off by Bob's insensitive approach. Bob defended himself by saying that he was frustrated by her unresponsiveness and, in his deprivation, came on too strong. They were locked into this kind of nonproductive cycle of charge and countercharge until Bob began to see another side of himself. He knew his heavy-handed way of making sexual overtures turned Jane off. Why then was he allowing his frustration to perpetuate this self-defeating behavior? What possible advantage could he be receiving?

The clue lay in the fact that Bob withdrew to his office after Jane refused him. Now he could get at his work without feeling guilty for neglecting her. After all, since she had resisted his overtures, he was justified in his withdrawal. Behind this marital problem was the familiar phenomenon of the double-mind.

Bob's conflict is related to a common way we avoid facing our double-mindedness. "If I weren't so busy," we say, "I would be able to get to these other important things." Busyness then is a way of satisfying both minds. "I'd like to—but I'm too busy." What happens when we are not too busy? Would it not be reasonable to suppose we would take the opportunity to get at "these other things?" The chances are, however, that resistance from our other mind will move us to distract ourselves from them until we are soon again too busy—and thereby protected. When we have "I want" and "I don't want" battling within us, and we acknowledge the "I want" and keep the "I don't want" hidden, the latter usually wins out by diverting the "I want" from its objectives. It is less likely to be detected because it functions in a way that is hidden.

When we are double-minded about our actions, we hope to solve the dilemma by "having our cake and eating it too." Of course, it cannot be done, but illusions are more easily accepted when we need to deny reality. If a married person is having an affair, for example, he or she may not want to make a choice between the lover and the marriage and family. Tom was in this bind. His relationship with Sue began as the two of them discovered they enjoyed each other's company, but before either was willing to acknowledge what was happening, it happened— they fell in love. But Tom had a wife and family that he respected and valued.

His involvement with Sue was a direct threat to his marriage, but Tom did not want to face this because he did not want to make a choice. People like Tom may subconsciously hope that something will happen to decide *for* them, and so they continue unrealistically on their collision course. Although they may not be thinking in religious categories, they nonetheless hope that a super power will blast open a way through what appears to be an impenetrable barrier. In this respect, they have succumbed to the second temptation of Jesus, over which he was victorious. The tempter told Jesus to jump from the temple steeple and trust the Lord to protect him. Jesus replied, "You shall not tempt the Lord your God" (Matt. 4:5–7). In contrast, Tom and those in similar situations take the jump and then expect God to protect them from the consequences. After the die is cast—and they themselves have done the casting—they hope a super power will change it.

Double Signals

In our double-mindedness we may also be giving double signals. Most of us at one time or another have been on the receiving end of these double signals. Friends may say, "I don't want to go," when something tells us they are also saying, "I do." Or there are people who invite us to accompany them when we are not sure they really want us to accept. You probably have given your share of these confused signals.

Parents seem particularly prone to give such signals in dealing with their children. Family therapist Virginia Satir told the following story in a recent lecture. A young mother complained to Satir that she could not get her little girl to obey her. The therapist sensed her doubleness as the mother explained, "My little girl is so full of energy and spunk that it's hard to control her."

"You admire her spunk and energy, don't you?" Virginia asked. "I guess I do," said the mother. "She's so different from me in that respect."

Virginia explained to her that children need boundaries for their protection and not as punishment. "Don't play jokes with her when you mean it," she said. "Because you like her strong-mindedness, you may be giving double signals when you state the limits. First you need to come to terms with your ambivalence and then we can devise ways to move the child to accept your limits."

The young mother was saying, "Don't," but the admiration in her eyes was implying, "Do"! Her don't was then actually giving the child permission to do. A teenager leaving for a party was told by his father, "Don't do anything I wouldn't do." The youth was bemused by the advice. "What's he telling me to do?" he asked a friend.

The double signal behind the familiar "grow up" may be "don't"! Why? Because as a parent I also need you to stay the same—to be the child I have adjusted to and complain about—to be the projection for my anxiety, resentment, and irritation. Otherwise I will have to look elsewhere for a focus for these—or even worse, look inside myself to see the source. Besides, how could I function as a parent if you *did* grow up? How else can I relate to you—after all these years?

Spouses also may exchange double messages. Carl Whitaker says that the married person who says to his or her spouse, "Don't tell me if you are having an affair," is really giving the spouse permission to have one.

Double Life

Double-mindedness may lead also to a double life. Instead of simply occupying the same person, the opposing minds may become associated with two contrasting social environments that must not, dare not, meet. Robert Louis Stevenson's novel *Dr. Jekyll and Mr. Hyde* is a literary classic of this double life. The good Dr. Jekyll practices medicine by day and becomes at night the evil predator Mr. Hyde. The pejorative *hypocrite* is used to describe a person whose double life has been exposed. It is applied particularly to those who are ostensibly religious and moral but whose less conspicuous ways are something other. The familiar excuse that clergy hear when they invite people to attend church services is that there are too many hypocrites in the church. The word means, literally, "one who is hidden under." Jesus used it in his warning to the Pharisees, whom in their outwardly religiousness he compared to "whitewashed tombs, which outwardly appear beautiful, but within they are full of dead men's bones and all uncleanness. So you . . . . are full of hypocrisy and iniquity" (Matt. 23:27–28). The preoccupation with image building among those desiring to ascend the ladder of leadership in the social, economic, or political arena is a blatant acceptance of the priority of appearance over substance.

Those who live double lives must "cover their tracks" with deception. This in turn takes its toll on their self-image and on their intimate relationships. If one is not trustworthy, how can one trust? If one fears exposure because of what is hidden, how can one be intimate with another in any genuine way? A member of the clergy who had left the parish ministry for a specialized ministry in which he associated primarily with people of other professions said, "I find it liberating not to have to talk like a Christian." I wonder if his parishioners ever suspected?

It is a strain to live a double life. Joyce was to all appearances a happily married woman. Yet she had been having an increasingly intimate relationship with a less than happily married man who lived in the same apartment complex. When the neighbor's wife found out about the affair, she not only confronted Joyce but also Joyce's husband. It was a traumatic moment to say the least. Yet Joyce's reaction indicated it was something else. "I was relieved," she said. The strain of the hiddenness—of evading reality—was over!

Yet the strain of living a double life is only an intensification of the strain of having a double mind. One may want also to have relief from that strain. How then to achieve this? How can we come to grips with our dividedness so that we can—at least now and then—experience wholeness? In wholeness our energy can be devoted to single-minded efforts, rather than being divided by the power struggle within; instead of being chronically indecisive, we can make up our minds. It is this quest for integration that is the thrust—the focus—of this book.

Do You Want It?

Before we can begin to work toward achieving single-mindedness, we need to raise three preliminary questions. The first of these concerns a possible double-mindedness about overcoming double-mindedness itself. Do you *want* to become united behind your desires? This may sound like a stupid question. Why wouldn't you? Because there may be some advantage in staying the way you are.

So ask yourself the question and evaluate your answer. Motivation—single-mindedness—about what you want is the first step to receiving it.

Yet one needs to raise the question with a full realization of the difficulties one faces. Living can be painful once we cease to protect our desires by our double-mindedness. When Jack committed himself for treatment of his chemical dependency, for example, he believed he wanted to overcome his addiction. But when he faced the pain of self-examination in the fourth and fifth steps of AA, he was not so sure. "I'm scared," he said. "I don't know whether I can take it." "Of course it is frightening," I said. "You now have a decision to make. Will you permit fear to dominate your life or will you choose to go through the ordeal for the sake of the sobriety that is on the other side?"

The second preliminary question grows out of the options just presented. Do you *believe* you can do it? Or is there double-mindedness about this also? In the Cancer Counseling and Research Center in Fort Worth, Texas, the physicians and therapists consider this question critical for healing. Yet even a positive answer may not tell the whole story. Because in our culture cancer is associated with death, it is difficult to know whether a positive ansewr to the question is given for the sake of those around the patient or whether it is a true reflection of the patient's own vision. "When patients verbalize a positive expectancy, saying they are not going to die or they are going to 'beat this thing,' " observes researcher Carl Simonton, "and yet crawl into bed and pull the covers over their heads, don't go to work, and exhibit other behavior incompatible with what they are saying, it is apparent to us they do not really have a firm belief that they can get well."[2]

Double-mindedness can be challenged, but it takes faith to believe it if you have experienced only failure in this regard. Yet as Jesus said repeatedly, it is our faith that makes us whole. Our expectations exert more influence upon our efforts than we normally realize.

The third preliminary question concerns those with whom you live or with whom you associate. Can you accept the possibility that your family and your friends may not support you in your efforts to change? This does not mean that they are not really your friends. Rather it means that they, like you, may be double-minded about who they want you to be. As mentioned previously, the balance in the family may depend on your keeping your problem. The question must be asked simply to prepare you for the eventuality that the support you anticipate may be surprisingly absent, and often at critically important times. It will take your family and friends time to adjust to changes in you that they actually—at least with one of their minds—desire. This throws you back once again on your own motivation for change.

Assuming that on the basis of these preliminary inquiries you are ready to move ahead, we will explore first the role that doubt plays in our double-mindedness.

2

Debilitating Doubt

The letter of James compares double-mindedness with doubting. In the context of encouraging those who lack wisdom to ask God for it, James emphasizes *how* one should ask. "Let him ask in faith, with no doubting." How we ask determines to some extent whether or not we will receive. Doubting is a hindrance to receiving. "He who doubts is like a wave of the sea that is driven and tossed by the wind." Doubting is being double-minded. The doubter, James says, "must not suppose that a double-minded man, unstable in all his ways, will receive anything from the Lord" (James 1:6–8).

Two Kinds of Doubt

There are actually two kinds of doubt. The first kind can be labeled intellectual doubt. It is faith's natural tension, implicit in Søren Kierkegaard's description of faith as a *leap*. The shadows are present but one acts in spite of them. Although we live in a tangible world in which we function through our senses, our faith is in a God who cannot be seen with our eyes or heard with our ears or touched with our hands. Intellectual doubt is the tension inherent in this difference. When atheist Madalyn Murray O'Hair accuses Christians of doubting the existence of God, she is referring to this tension of faith with intellectual doubt.

Christian apologist C. S. Lewis was an atheist until he was thirty years of age. During this period he was not spared the discomfort of doubting. Maybe his atheism was wrong! Maybe God *is*! When he became a Christian he did not cease to doubt; rather his faith and doubt exchanged places. Now that he had affirmed his faith in God, he had doubts about whether his Christian affirmation was right. Yet he did not *believe* his doubts. If he had, his doubt would have become his faith.

This relationship of faith with intellectual doubt is comparable to that of courage with fear. If you did something really dangerous and did not know of the danger, your act could scarcely be called courageous. In fact, should you later realize the danger you were in, you might begin to shake with retroactive fear. But if you knew of the danger and experienced the fear that went with this realization, and yet acted in spite of it, that would be courageous. So also your faith may be all the more *faith*ful when it is affirmed in spite of its painful tension with doubt. Intellectual doubt, therefore, is a potential stimulus to faith. We leap, not being sure where we will land—except that we are leaping in the direction of our faith.

The other kind of doubt prevents us from making such a leap. It does not center in our intellect but in our total person; so it is frequently called self-doubt. We are divided within ourselves and actually program ourselves for defeat. We are too double-minded to move in any one direction, and so we are beaten before we start. It is this self-doubt to which James refers when he says that he who doubts is like a wave of the sea, driven and tossed by the wind.

Our Lives Have Become Unmanageable

In self-doubt we are at variance with ourselves—hesitant within ourselves. There are many colloquial expressions describing this hesitancy. "She doesn't know what she wants." "He can't get his head together." "She's only partially in what she's doing." "He can't make up his mind." In such a divided state, we are not open to receive even what we supposedly ask for and want. Rather, we are driven and tossed by opposing forces within "like a wave of the sea." Even if we do make a decision in this divided state, we doubt if we have made the right decision and so continue to be uncertain and confused. We are simply not confident enough to affirm without hedging.

Some people are chronic hedgers. When you ask them direct questions, they qualify their answers with "I guess," "I suppose so," or "maybe," "perhaps," "possibly," "it could be," or "I'm not sure." When I am counseling people who hedge in these ways I draw it to their attention. A typical dialogue would go like this.

> *Counselor:* Bob, you indicated that it upsets you if your wife leaves you alone at parties.
> *Bob:* Yeah—I guess so.
> *Counselor:* How do you mean "guess"?
> *Bob:* Well—yes it does. I just hate to admit it, I guess.
> *Counselor:* You "guess"?
> *Bob (laughing):* There I go again!

"Let not the hesitant and hedging suppose that they shall receive, for a double-minded person is unstable in all his or her ways" (James 1:8, paraphrase). The Greek word translated "unstable," *akatastatos*, is composed of three root words, *a-kata-istemi*, and means literally, "not according to one's being." An unstable person, therefore, is one who is not in charge of him or herself—is out of control. One's inner self is in a state of anarchy. The condition is best described by the First Step of Alcoholics Anonymous, "Our lives have become unmanageable." In such a state one lacks identity, having no unity of will and therefore no freedom.

The word *unmanageable* is contrasted with *discipline*. Again, the root words help our understanding. *Manage* comes from *manus*, which means "in hand," that is, "having things in hand." *Unmanageable* would then describe a situation where "things are out of hand." *Discipline* comes from *discipulus*, meaning "learner," particularly one whose learning leads to self-development and self-management. The word *disciple* comes from the same root.

The Opposing Mind

Double-mindedness implies an opposing mind, often unacknowledged. In Book VIII of his *Confessions*, St. Augustine is bemused over "a great mystery." The mind can tell the body what to do—"Raise your hand"—and up goes the hand. But the mind can tell the mind what to do—such as to concentrate or to prepare an assignment—and nothing may happen. Is not the mind closer to itself than it is to the body? In fact, should not the very act of the mind's directing itself be the same as carrying it out?

In reflecting on this mystery, Augusting concludes that perhaps he has been under an illusion, namely, that he has one mind. What if there are *two* minds? Then the mystery would clear. For what the one mind has the other would lack, and what the one wanted the other would resist.

Augustine provides an example of his own two minds concerning hs well-known sexual difficulties, by making a parody of his prayer: "Give me chastity and continency—but not yet!" Double-mindedness, or self-doubting, occurs when one of our minds opposes the other.

The word translated as double-minded in James is *disuchos*, which is literally "two souled." *Double-minded*, therefore, does not refer to mind as intellect, or even as reason, but to mind as soul or psyche. The description "two souled," of course, is psychological and not ontological. Goethe used this description when he had Faust say, "Two souls dwell, alas! in my breast."

The analogy of double-mindedness to a wave of the sea that is driven and tossed by the wind corresponds to the clinical term for double-mindedness coined by Freud, namely, *ambivalence*. *Ambivalence (ambi-valence)* means literally "both strengths," or "two opposing strengths." An ambivalent person is one who is driven and tossed by conflicting forces within. The two strengths—minds, souls, psyches—do not speak to each other, nor are they reconciled with each other. They may not even be aware of each other.

Reaction to External Pressures

In his description of doubting as being driven and tossed like a wave of the sea by the wind, James emphasizes the external pressures that bear upon us. There are many things that happen to us that put pressure on us to doubt. The crucial point is our internal susceptibility to these pressures.

In the ancient Biblical story of the Fall of Man, the serpent-tempter seduces Eve to eat the forbidden fruit by subtly planting a doubt. "Did God say, 'You shall not eat of any tree of the garden'?" (Gen. 3:1). In confirming that this is what God had said, the woman reported the warning that should she disobey, she would die. Challenging this threat, the tempter pointed instead to the advantages of eating the fruit, thus sowing the suspicion that God wanted to keep her from these advantages. "You will not die. For God knows that when you eat of it your eyes will be opened, and you will be like God, knowing good and evil" (Gen. 3:4–5). To be like God! Eve was vulnerable to the pressure. Fascinated by the attractiveness of the fruit—it was "a delight to her eyes"—she finally ate it (Gen. 3:6). The tempter had simply exploited her own double-mindedness.

I often see this double-mindedness under the guise of "honest doubting" in my counseling. Phil, for example, was faced with the dilemma of either studying in a concentrated way for a final examination or failing it and facing dismissal from his graduate program. As he reflected on what had to be done to pass the exam, he said, "I doubt that I can do it." The implication, of course, was that he lacked the resources. "I've fallen so far behind in my reading," he explained, "that now I'm finding it next to impossible to concentrate." Both getting far behind in his assignments and finding it next to impossible to concentrate indicate that Phil was resisting what he was doing. Perhaps he was inwardly divided over whether he wanted to be in the profession for which he was preparing. Or he may have doubted whether he had the ability and sabotaged his efforts because he questioned his "competency."

In Phil's case it turned out to be the latter. "Everybody has always told me that I had the ability," he said, "even when all I was doing was enough to get by. I guess I was afraid to go all out—afraid maybe I didn't really *have* what is takes. Now in graduate school it's caught up with me. I'm not getting by anymore."

Phil's doubt about whether he had ability grew out of his double-mindedness over finding out. "I go through such a struggle trying to study." he said. But who was he struggling with? Himself!

As Phil indicated, doubting is not only debilitating, it is also agonizing. One is driven and tossed—buffeted—by opposing forces or strengths within oneself. John the Baptist, for example, had announced confidently that he was sent by God to prepare the way for the Messiah. He performed that function as one who "knew his own mind." He pointed to Jesus saying, "Behold the lamb of God, who takes away the sin of the world!" (John 1:29). Then he was imprisoned by Herod the king for his denunciation of Herod's immoral conduct. Languishing in Herod's dungeon, facing the likelihood of execution, he was disturbed by doubts. Had he been right in his convictions? If so, why was he now forsaken? Was he really the forerunner of the Messiah and was Jesus really the Messiah?

When one is facing the end of life it is devastating to doubt the validity of what one has done with it. As a way of resolving his doubt, John sent two of his own disciples to Jesus with a question: "Are you he who is to come, or shall we look for another?" (Luke 7:19). Jesus could have been offended, but he understood the pressures on John and gave him the support he needed. Since he was healing the sick and the afflicted when John's disciples arrived, he said, "Go and tell John what you have seen and heard: the blind receive their sight, the lame walk, lepers are cleansed, and the deaf hear, the dead are raised up, the poor have good news preached to them. And blessed is he who takes no offense at me" (Luke 7:22–23). Not only was this an impressive array of "signs," but these were signs associated in the Old Covenant with messianic activity (see Isa. 35:5–6), and John would so recognize them.

Doubting undermines our confidence as we lose whatever nerve we had. In our concern over the possibility of failure, we hesitate to take any risks. Despite the jokes about those who aspire to "walk on the water," the story of Saint Peter's attempt is a pointed illustration of the debilitating effects of doubt. When Peter "saw the wind" he "was afraid" and began "to sink." As Jesus reached out and grabbed his hand he said, "O man of little faith, why did you doubt?" (Matt. 14:30–31). As long as he kept his eyes on the beckoning Christ, he was in control, but when he looked instead to the threatening wind and waves, he lost that control to fear. When we focus our attention on the negative—that is, on the frightening possibilities that surround us and that threaten our survival—we are by that very focus stimulating our doubt.

Doubt disrupts our integration. It is the dark and menacing shadow that undermines our courage. Actually it is not doubt but doubting that does the damage. Doubting is something we *do*, not just something we *have*; it is an undermining activity, "chipping away" at our sense of self-worth. How then do we cease this destructive pursuit?

A Confrontation Between Two Souls

Since doubting is an action that reflects our inner division, we need to bring our "opposing souls" together as a first step toward integration. Since such a confrontation is painful, we tend to avoid it. Yet there is potential healing in our facing directly our unacceptable soul or self—our opposing mind. Like his cousin John, Jesus also had his time of devastating stress. The external pressure in his case (as in John's) was his impending execution. In the garden of Gethsemane on the eve of his crucifixion, he too began to question his mission. "Father," he prayed, "if it be possible, let this cup pass from me" (Matt. 26:39). The "cup" was the symbol of the suffering he had previously said was his destiny as the Messiah. Now that it was upon him, he was inwardly in turmoil. His prayer was an expression of his doubting.

Both Jesus and John dealt openly with their doubts. They went to the source of the problem. John in his forsakenness doubted whether he was right in pointing to Jesus as the Messiah. He took those doubts to Jesus with a request for help. Jesus in his forsakenness doubted whether his calling really included such suffering, or if it did, whether he could endure it. He took his doubts to God in an anguishing night of prayer. His initial petition expressed his honest desire to "cop out." Once this mind (or soul, or self) had been expressed, the other came forth. "My Father, if this cannot pass unless I drink it, thy will be done" (Matt. 26:42).

Both John and Jesus worked through their doubting—and not around it—by communicating it to the one it primarily concerned. Jesus came to a decision and the implication is that John did also. Jesus was, in effect, going through the same kind of experience as the father of the demon-possessed boy when he was devastated by his son's suffering and the inability of Jesus' disciples to help him. "If you can do anything, have pity on us and help us," he cried out. Jesus responded to his doubting. "If you can! All things are possible to him who believes." Challenged by this to affirm himslf, the father responded with his own anguished prayer: "I believe; help my unbelief!" (Mark 9:22–24).

Some ancient manuscripts state that after Jesus worked through his doubts to a decision, "there appeared an angel from heaven strengthening him." He needed this strengthening because he had chosen not to evade the cross. It is not coincidental that his strengthening came *after* he had reached a decision. Once we affirm our identity, our calling, the resulting integration opens us to receive. We have, as it were, "crossed the sound barrier," and from then on our energy can be used to support us in the direction we have chosen. We can reach out to ask others for their assistance; we can pray for help and be specific in our petitions.

3

When Fear Takes Over

Having described how double-mindedness and its counterpart, doubt, operate, we need now to look into what causes them. The first of such causes that we shall explore is fear. The ancient story of the Exodus is a dramatic illustration of how fear can create double-mindedness. After several mighty signs of the Lord's favor, the Hebrew people escaped from their Egyptian captivity to go to their "promised land." It was the vision of this land that inspired them in their arduous journey; yet when they finally arrived, they refused to enter. What had undermined their desire?

Immobilized by Fear

The closer they came to their destination, the more they began to fear the actual conquest of the land. They had known from the beginning that they could not just "walk in"; there were people living there who considered the land their own. But that was far into the future. Now that it was at hand they grew apprehensive. So they chose twelve persons to spy out the land. On their return, ten of them reflected the fears of the people. The land, they said, "devours its inhabitants" (Num. 13:32).

Two of the spies—Caleb and Joshua—disagreed. "Let us go up at once and occupy it," they said, "for we are well able to overcome it" (Num. 13:30). But once they had become frightened, the people could not hear them. Caleb and Joshua tried to reason with them. "The Lord is with us, do not fear them" (Num. 14:9). In appealing to trust they were pointing to the antidote for fear. Yet reason is no match for panic. Have you ever tried to "push" people to act when they were frightened? What happened? They probably turned on you in anger. Anger is often the last desperate defense of the frightened. When Caleb and Joshua persisted, the mood of the people turned ugly. "Stone them with stones," they shouted (Num. 14:10).

Though anger may reflect our fear, we look anything but frightened when we are angry. In fact, anger gives the impression of strength. People who speak—or shout—angrily tend to intimidate. But it is all based on the athletic coach's philosophy that the best defense is a good offense. Not only may anger be a sign of fear, it may also be a sign of self-doubt. The Hebrew people must have known in the depths of their souls that Caleb and Joshua were right. But the truth was too much to hear, let alone to bear. Their anger was evidence of their determination to deny the truth. Refusing to enter their promised land, they ended up wandering in the wilderness for the rest of their lives.

Fear as Timidity

The fear that causes double-mindedness shows itself primarily as timidity. Debilitating our confidence, making us hesitant to act, this timidity, says the Second Letter to Timothy, is no gift of God; in fact, timidity's opposite would be God's gift. "God did not give us a spirit of timidity but a spirit of power and love and self-control" (2 Tim. 1:7). Self-control might better be translated self-direction, since self-control may today be interpreted as "keeping the lid on." The King James Version uses the words sound mind. Sound in this sense means "healthy" or "integrated"—a mind that can direct itself. It is the opposite of the unstable mental state characteristic of double-mindedness. A synonym for sound, healthy, or integrated is single, meaning "honest and genuine." The Greek word *sophronismos* of which all of these are possible translations means literally a "disciplined mind," one that is committed to one's duty or calling.

Fear gets in the way of our commitment or calling. The fear of assertion, of risking, can so divide our mind that we may become immobilized. Instead of being integrated around a commitment, a duty, a calling, we timidly back away from such assertion, seeking instead the illusion of safety.

Safety is an illusion because these retreating tactics are in the direction of death. In fact, the things that we fear are usually symbols of death.As Virginia Satir says, "The fear of making mistakes, the fear of being wrong—any fear for that matter—can get tied up with death."³ Like death, each of these fearful possibilities threatens to "do us in." We are not sure we could survive. Obviously, this withdrawal is a retreat from life rather than from death, and is therefore an illusional way of salvation. The fear of death is normal; we fear any terminus to our being. The question, therefore, is how do we cope with this fear? By facing the reality of what threatens us or by avoiding it? Once we come to grips with the certainty of our own death and deal realistically with it, we are in a better position to affirm life, since the basic risk to it has been accepted.

Universality of Fear

Fear is a good and necessary passion and all of us have it. It is a "feeling" response to a threatening situation and is basically for our protection. Fear provides the tension we need to act quickly, and can be an expression of a united mind.

The problem with fear is that we can fear the wrong thing. For example, people who fear to say anything about injustice in their midst because of what may happen to them socially or economically or professionally may jeopardize something more important, namely, their personal integrity. It is this potential loss that they should fear. Or we can be afraid of bringing up sensitive issues that need to be talked about in our intimate relationships because we are not sure how our initiative will be received, and be far less fearful of the horrendous possibility of nuclear war, the potentiality of which is too mind-boggling even to contemplate.

Because so many of our fears are holdovers from a previous time in our lives and are irrational in their present setting, we need to ask ourselves what it is specifically that we fear. This may be difficult to sort out, since our anxieties tend to focus on the more visible, surface issues. Consequently, we need to go beyond these to get to the core of our fears. It may help to imagine the worst that you might anticipate in any threatening situation. When you have identified this, ask yourself whethere it is really the most dreadful thing that could happen to you in this situation, or whether there is something even more dreadful if you consider the potential loss in terms of values associated with your growth as a person and your care for others. Jack, the chemically dependent person mentioned in a previous chapter who feared the treatment program as much as he did his addiction, had to do this deeper probing. As he looked more closely into his resistance he realized what he actually feared the most. "I'm terrified at being on the hot seat. I'm scared to death of those guys in the group."

Like Jack, some of us may be fearing the wrong thing. What we often fear most is the pain that is necessary for our own growth. In allowing this fear to dominate us, we are opting for a stunted existence in which our potential for development is forfeited. It is an awful choice! We need to face up to the power we have to choose. Realizing that we have a choice may be a sobering enough awareness to dislodge our fear.

I asked Jack what he would like to see as his first priority rather than his fear. Without much reflection, he answered, "Trust." In saying this he not only revealed his double mind but also his awareness that trust was what he lacked. Significantly, trust is the opposite of fear, and Jack intuitively or subconsciously perceived this.

Jesus repeatedly contrasted trust and fear. A typical example was the question he put to his disciples while at sea when they awakened him in panic because of the storm that was threatening to upset their boat. "Why are you afraid, O men of little faith?" (Matt. 8:26). In his first inaugural address, Franklin Delano Roosevelt attempted to reassure a panicking people in the midst of the Great Depression by saying, "The only thing we have to fear is fear itself." Singling out fear itself rather than the objects of fear takes us to the source of the problem. But we still need a resource to cope with this fear—and this resource is trust.

Fear Inhibits Communication

Fear can prevent us from communicating in our significant relationships. For example, one of the conclusions of two well-known therapists in their years of assisting couples with sexual problems is that married couples tend not to talk with each other about their sexual needs or frustrations. From my own counseling experience I know this to be true. Why should this be? Is it out of fear that one's spouse will not respond, or even worse, will explicitly reject the overtures of openness? Undoubtedly this is part of the problem. Perhaps, however, we are also afraid of our own desires, or are double-minded about our acceptance of them, and hesitate under these circumstances to reveal them, even—or especially—to our spouse. Besides the fear of what the other may think, there is the fear of being "known" by one from whom we cannot walk away—one to whom we are bonded.

Under such circumstances, it takes courage to take the initiative and open the subject. Such courage, of course, is the opposite of timidity. Our double-mindedness is aggravated by the fear that we will not succeed. We fear the power of the other to deny us what we desire. Consequently, we need to face this potential limitation, and as a psychiatrist friend of mine says, give the other person the freedom to say yes or no. Then we are liberated from the necessity to succeed and so can make the overture with less risk to our self-esteem. This, in turn, makes it easier to take the initiative.

Courage alone is not enough, however. We also need wisdom. The initiative needs to be taken at the right time, at the right place, and in the right manner. If we are insensitive to any of these, the other person may not be able to hear accurately what we are saying. It is wise also to "do our homework" prior to taking this initiative. We can detract from an otherwise effective approach by having our facts wrong or by being unaware of pertinent information. To be convincing, we need to be accurate and informed.

In our fearfulness, we may lack the faith to believe that our overture will succeed. Unfortunately this may predispose it to fail; our anticipations do have an effect on the outcome, and fear is a particularly powerful predisposing factor. Kierkegaard points out that the dread of something—such as sin—can actually lead a person into it. Faith, on the other hand, provides the resource to project a positive anticipation into the endeavor. It is an even more powerful factor for the positive than fear is for the negative. It is because love includes faith that "love . . . believes all things, hopes all things" (1 Cor. 13:7).

Our positive anticipation does not guarantee success, however, any more than do other assets, like sensitivity and wisdom. Therefore, we need to ask ourselves whether we have the internal security or fortitude necessary for enduring a negative outcome. When we "stick out our neck" to open communication and are rebuffed, we may be humiliated—unless we are humble enough to accept the defeat. Our trust need not disintegrate because of the failure. God is still God and our identity is still in him. One never knows whether the apparent failure will have a later useful purpose. It could be a transitional event behind which God is hidden. So we need to maintain our hopeful perspective. In the meantime, the same love that hopes all things also "endures all things," bears all things," even the disappointment over a venture that has apparently failed.

Breaking the Domination of Fear

Because fear is such an overwhelming passion, only those who are strongly motivated to do so can break its domination. This motivation comes from the other mind. Our reason itself is no match for fear; we must be motivated to be free of fear's domination. While motivation does not make one omnipotent, it does provide a formidable power for change. Masters and Johnson, for example, assert that one of the most difficult of human changes, namely, the change from a strong homosexual preference to a heterosexual preference, is possible, but only possible if the person involved is sufficiently motivated. Such motivation, in essence, constitutes single-mindedness.

Instances of single-mindedness come about, of course, in the midst of double-mindedness. We make a conscious choice to back one of these minds and to disregard the other. Usually this conscious choice is based on the belief that our best interests lie in this direction. In other words, we care enough for ourselves to "blow the whistle" on our destructive tendencies and consciously make a decision, rather than letting the consequences of double-mindedness make it for us. The key to such decision making is a sense of self-worth. When this is lacking, there may be insufficient ego strength to withhold present satisfaction, even though it threatens one's hopes for the future. When we really care about ourselves, that is, when we have a sense of self-worth, we are concerned about how we will feel after the present satisfaction as well as during it.

When asked about this choice, people who are oriented only to present satisfaction will usually say, "I don't think about the future—I don't consider it." On the surface, this may sound like a sensible approach, since the future is not here and the present is. Those who are concerned only about the future may never live in the present. Yet the fact remains that the future has a way of becoming the present. When it comes, we may ruefully regret the choices that predisposed us to our now-present misery. We can be double-minded about caring for ourselves if it means giving up something we desire in the present so that we may have more of what we desire in some future "present." In these critical moments, we need to ask ourselves whether it is really ourselves we care about or just the momentary experience of ease or pleasure.

The story of Esau in the Old Testament is a story of one who exemplified the latter. Although he was the hunter in the family and physically strong, he had little inner strength compared to his physically weaker brother, Jacob. Jacob consequently knew how to manipulate him. When Esau returned from a hunting trip famished, he wanted the food his brother was preparing. Jacob saw his chance. "First sell me your birthright." Preoccupied with his hunger pangs, Esau said, "I am about to die; of what use is the birthright to me?" Jacob forced the bargain: "Swear to me first" (Gen. 25:31–33). So Esau swore and surrendered his birthright. Later he deeply regretted his decision and hated his brother for exploiting his weakness, but it was too late. Jacob had all the advantages, then, of the older son. So, like Esau, we can sell our birthright for a morsel of meat. The issue in any moment of double-mindedness is what kind of consequences do we want to live with? For live with them we shall!

When we decide for larger goals instead of for immediate satisfaction, pleasure, ease, or safety, we feel good about ourselves. This is a reward in itself. We know we have accomplished something, experienced a victory, and we sense a new source of power—a spirit of self-direction. In contrast to these gains, the no-risk security that we achieve by our timid backing away from scary new possibilities is indeed a paltry acquisition. In fact, we dislike ourselves even more when we give in to the fears and desires of the moment. As the future becomes the present, we are disappointed with ourselves for our weakness and timidity.

The low self-worth that stimulated our fears is only intensified when we succumb to them. The way to single-mindedness lies in breaking through the fear barrier. It is like getting into the water. The hard part is going from the warm beach into the cold water, and the next hard part is staying in the water until we become acclimated to our new environment. After a while the heretofore frigid water actually begins to be comfortable—even exhilarating. We feel good not only about the water but about ourselves.

The fear that divides us—and provides the double mind with its power to sabotage—is essentially the fear of ourselves. Trusting God must lead ultimately to trusting ourselves. We need to be reconciled with who we are to counteract our fear of the monster we envision as ourselves in our self-estrangement.

4

Getting Down on Yourself

Conflicts with Our Goals and Desires

The load of unresolved guilt that many of us carry within ourselves is another cause of double-mindedness. Our misgivings over ourselves can conflict with our goals and desires. What we desire for ourselves may seem too much for "the likes of us". Considering who I am—who am I to have such goals?

Some of us may feel more comfortable "snitching" something than in receiving it as a gift. We justify our taking something from another by our resentment against supposed injustices; yet were this same something offered to us as a gift, we might feel undeserving in receiving it. This discrepancy between what our self-image can tolerate and what is offered to us may make us feel too unworthy to receive. Yet this same low self-image may make us resentful enough to seize—by stealth or force.

This uncomfortableness with receiving is especially so when the gift is unconditional love. As Kierkegaard has observed, we can actually be offended by this love because it is "too high" for us. The gift of love is offered obviously to our person, concerning which we tend to feel the most inadequate. We simply do not deserve it because in our own eyes we are too unlovable. So we try to compensate for our unlovable person by producing or accomplishing something that will make us more qualified to receive this "gift." We are conditioned, it seems, to conditional love and consequently try to meet the supposedly necessary conditions.

This down-on-myself state of mind, described clinically as a low self-image, results from the accumulation of unresolved guilt. Developmental psychologist Erik Erikson describes it as shame. Our shame, he says, concerns our being, and our guilt concerns our doing, or lack of doing. One feels shame over being who one is—"incompetent," "distorted," "perverted," "inadequate," "worthless." When this is the case, one's self-image is obviously low.

Low is a comparative term. Its opposite would be high, although one seldom hears the term high self-image; usually the comparison is with a healthy, or good, self-image. We judge ourselves low when we are not living up to the expectations that we impose on ourselves. These expectations come originally from what we perceived as the expectations of others concerning us. Once we have internalized them, however, we tend to bear down on ourselves even harder than did those original persons who supposedly expected so much—and were disappointed.

A low self-image is really low self-esteem—again, a comparative term. As we see ourselves in comparison, or even in competition, with others, we may come out rather poorly. Of course, this is a fluctuating perception, for through specific achievements or compliments, we may go up in our estimation. Because it is dependent in this fluctuating way on getting "strokes" from others, Rational Emotive therapist Albert Ellis thinks we should give up our pursuance of self-esteem. Besides, having esteem is not the advantage is is touted to be. "What we call esteem," he says, "often amounts to self-aggrandizement, for we often tend to feel ourselves as better or more worthy than other people."[4] I tend to agree with Ellis. It is not self-esteem that we need but self-worth.

Worth as a Gift

Self-worth is neither comparative nor achievable. We do not need accomplishments to prove ourselves as worthful persons. In fact, accomplishments cannot give us worth since they relate to our abilities. Unfortunately, when we consider our worth as an achievement rather than a gift, we are coerced into trying to establish it through accomplishments of one sort or another. But it will not work, because we are really pursuing self-esteem.

We can affirm our self-worth only because this worth is essentially a gift. Our cultural values are based on the illusion that this worth must be achieved through our sundry accomplishments. In contrast, the Gospel is Good News precisely because it releases us from this pressure by affirming our worth as a gift from God. Our baptism is God's seal of this gift, the symbolic rite of its reception.

But God is not an indulgent giver. The receiver has responsibilities with regard to the gift. Since God's gift of worth is not based on our being qualified for it but on our being accepted and loved as we are, we need have no fears about losing it. The Gospel is a help in coping with our perfectionist tendencies. When we are influenced by the cultural illusion that our worth has to be achieved, we have a natural defensiveness against any risk to our accomplishments. The fear of failure is in reality the fear of worthlessness. Any venture that exposes us to possible negative feedback sends the shivers through our soul. We find ourselves in a never ending entrapment, for what evaluation other than perfection can guarantee us our sense of worth? Particularly since in our insecurity we focus more on what we lack than on what we have!

In contrast, when we believe we are accepted as we are—that we possess our worth as a gift of God—we can afford to risk in our ventures, since the evaluation of these ventures is really no threat to us as persons. Whatever judgment may befall us, either from others or from ourselves, is transcended by the covenant of reconciliation in which we live. Under our cultural system the fear of rejection not only moves us to reject ourselves—to doubt our worth—but also to project this fear into our relationships with others. The judgment we pronounce on ourselves is usually more severe than the judgment we receive from others, however.

Realizing that our worth is a gift of God, we can become increasingly free of the stress that comes from trying to establish our worth in the competitive world. This freedom is also the freedom to venture, since our worth is not at stake in these ventures. These ventures, including their risks, lead to experiences that may enhance the gift. Our worth is a gift to be used. It is not to be "laid away in a napkin," like the pound of the servant in Jesus' parable who was afraid he might lose it. The judgment from his master was severe: "Why did you not put the money into the bank, and at my coming I should have collected it with interest?" (Luke 19:20–23).

Life with its gifts is not a static state; rather, it is always moving in one direction or another, always dynamic, always developing. Like the atoms that compose our bodies in submicroscopic particles, we as persons are in continuous motion. The only question is—in what direction are we moving? "For whoever would save his life [his worth] will lose it; and whoever loses his life [risks his worth] for my sake and the gospel's will save it [develop the gift]" (Mark 8:35).

As long as we are under the illusion that worth is esteem, our unresolved guilt will make us conspirators in undoing this esteem. Because of this double-mindedness about our esteem, we may contribute to our own failures, problems (including family problems), and even illnesses. Succeeding rather than failing, having peaceful relations rather than turbulent ones, and feeling well rather than ill may be too much for those whose guilt tells them they are unworthy or undeserving of such blessings. We want these benefits with one of our minds, but with the other we feel uneasy about them because they threaten the balance we need to maintain. Our guilt moves us to keep our debits and credits "balanced" in our "ledger." If the credits shoot up, this balance is broken. Better, we may feel, perhaps, to restore it ourselves through a bit of self-sabotage than to have it restored by powers beyond our own.

Restoring this balance ourselves also means staying in control, since control is very important for our security. Should we lose control, our destiny is in other hands. Subconsciously at least, we sense that these "other hands" are punitive and avenging. Better we remain in control, even if it means that we must suffer more pain. So long as the handicaps that we give ourselves are necessary for our security, we will hold on to them. When we no longer need them, that is, when we have a different basis for security—when we can entrust ourselves to hands other than our own—we can give them up.

For several years I was burdened with a painful knee. It was particularly painful one day as I was listening to a speech by Dr. Paul Brenner, a San Diego gynecologist who gave up his practice so that he could do what he wanted with his life. He had injured his own knee in a fall while jogging and had drugged himself with cortisone so that he could keep his speaking engagement. His several references to his painful knee made me more conscious of mine. I was discouraged over it, and when Brenner indicated that we tend to hold on to our chronic pains because we need them, I was irritated and expressed it. "Don't tell me I want this pain—that I'm holding on to it—because I just won't buy it." Brenner had said that the cortisone was making him less inhibited, and his response seemed to show it. "Whether you want to hear it or not, I believe you are holding on to it." His words sank into me, echoing as though spoken in a tunnel. As I pondered that experience, I decided in prayer that I would not need my pain any longer. Looking back on that encounter, I believe it was the beginning of what was still a long journey toward healing.

Our unresolved guilt binds us to our past. We have our old ways of doing things that are often ways by which we have learned to tolerate our existence. Though these ways are frequently self-defeating, they are still part of the qualifying system we have developed to compensate for our low self-esteem. Whether by inordinately hard work, or self-imposed deprivations, or self-inflicted or self-exacerbated suffering, we are searching for that toleration level at which we can feel deserving.

Reluctance to Make Decisions

Our guilt shows up also in our reluctance to make decisions. Actually, we are making decisions all the time, but we have a way of concealing this from ourselves. Although someone may make a decision for us, we still to some degree have permitted this to happen; our decision to do this is hidden behind our defensive belief that another has assumed this responsibility. Students studying for a profession like the ministry, for instance, may have some misgivings over their choice of career. Yet they may feel under obligation to continue in it. Because they would feel guilty if they made a decision to drop their studies, they may instead so conduct themselves that others will make that decision for them. In this way they resolve their double-mindedness. As a teacher, I have the impression on occasion that a student who seems prone to self-sabotage in the form of being delinquent in his or her studies may want to be dismissed.

A spouse wanting to end a marriage may likewise be unwilling to seek a divorce for fear of bringing judgment upon him or herself. Instead, he or she may make the marriage so unsatisfactory for the other that he or she will ultimately take that step.

Those engaging in extra-marital affairs are another case in point. Neither may be willing to admit responsibility for initiating the affair. For similar reasons, each may be equally reluctant to place this responsibility on the other. Instead, each may describe the affair as having "just happened." Nobody planned it, nobody initiated it; therefore nobody is responsible—except fate or whatever gods there be who engineer such "happenings." If no one is responsible, no one is guilty.

Even in less heavy matters many of us may be reluctant to assume responsibility. "He thought I should" or "she suggested it" are frequent ways in which we protect ourselves from being the one who has made the decision. Once we have openly decided we are responsible, and if responsible then vulnerable; we have put ourselves "on the line." There is no excuse, no defense, if the decision is proved wrong; we have "burned our bridges."

Since making a decision openly puts us potentially under judgment, whatever latent guilt we carry within us is activated, with all of its accompanying misery. Being highly sensitive to any such activation, we tend instead to back away from the danger. Security in such a moment lies in not being responsible, so that in whatever happens we can maintain our innocence. "It's not my fault!"

Most of our arguments with family or friends center in this defensiveness against responsibility. The charge and counter-charge dynamic that characterizes these heated exchanges boils down to each claiming innocence and directly or indirectly laying the major portion of blame on the other. Such arguments may even be instigated as an "offense" defense.

This fear of decision making may lead one to be double-minded over exercising a parental role. Yet, if and when we become parents, this is our role. Parents are leaders by virtue of being parents. Our children need us through the years of their development because they are unable to assume adult responsibilities. At the same time, children have minds of their own that may not always respond to their parents' leadership. In fact, they may actively resist this leaderhsip. If the parent has a guilty fear over being decisive, what happens to parental leadership when the issue at hand is controversial? How can parents who feel guilty over being decisive respond with what Dr. James Dobson calls "confident decisiveness"? Even if such parents do not abandon their leadership role but persist despite the threat, they will by this persistence activate their latent guilt.

We parents can be under the illusion—stemming from our guilt—that any intervention of ours that temporarily disrupts the harmony of our relationship with our child will do permanent harm, not only to the relationship but also to the child. This again is a projected judgment of our guilt. In our frustration over acting or not acting we would rather not be parental. Actually we would rather not be parents! We would feel more comfortable being friends or counselors, but it is a little late for that. If we do overcome our resistance and intervene, we often do so with more anger than is commensurate with the offense, simply because we are angry over having been "forced" to take action. After our confrontation with the child, we usually distance ourselves rather than move toward the child. We are, in effect, pouting, feeling sorry for ourselves for being trapped in our "angry" guilt.

Consequently, the important task of reassuring and teaching the child after the confrontation is left undone. If we parents could follow up the conflict with this reassurance, we would be likely to expose the illusion that the incident has caused irretrievable harm. My own tendency, as the reader may perceive, is very much as I have described. On one occasion, however, I did it differently. When my child was "getting on my nerves"—and perhaps knowingly so, since it was an old issue—I gave a firm directive for the behavior to cease. Since this occurred at a family outing, I would normally believe that I had ruined the potential perfection of the day, and I would withdraw in wrathful silence after the confrontation. This time, however, I did not. Instead, I moved warmly toward the child, and the incident was soon "over" for both of us. This was new parental ground for me, and it felt good.

Perhaps some of this resistance to parental decision making is also a reaction against a parental stance that we remember from our own homes. We may still be rebelling against our parents' authority as it is now internalized in our own psyche. When someone gives us an authoritative directive—"do it"—we impulsively react, "Oh yeah!" Should our double-mindedness over decision making join with a dated defiance of parental authority, the combination can prove very difficult to penetrate.

Fear of Exposure

Our unresolved guilt can also cause us to have an exaggerated fear of exposure. So long as our guiltiness is known only to ourselves, our ego has protection. To insure this protection, we become strongly defensive in our motivations. At the same time, the presence of our guilt makes us highly sensitive to criticism. Since our guilt carries its own judgment upon us, it does not take much for us to perceive such judgment coming from others. Sometimes we may actually project it onto them; we hear the accusation coming from another when in reality it is coming from within ourselves.

If through some event or circumstance our defense system is penetrated and our guilt, or rather whatever we feel guilty about, is exposed, we experience humiliation. When we are humiliated, we react with rage or depression. Actually, rage and depression may be combined in a dominant-recessive relationship. When one is depressed, one may not be aware of the rage that is combined with the depression, a rage against the apparent attack on one's self-esteem. So also, when one rages against another over being humiliated, one may not be aware of the depression contained in the rage.

I had a student who failed a very important test. That he would feel bad about this was only natural. But he did more than feel bad, he became depressed, and not just for a day but for many days. In his depression he believed that since he had failed in this important endeavor, he had failed as a person. Unable to separate his person from his activities, he was convinced he was no good, worthless, that he had nothing to offer. In spite of his "downness" he was not humble. Rather, his reaction was one of pride. He wanted—needed—a higher image of himself, and his failure had deprived him of this. His pride was wounded and this was the basis of his depression. In such depressions, one tends to indulge oneself with self-inflicted misery. The depression is essentially a form of protest, even though the focus is on pain. The rage implicit in the depression is expressed in rebelling against a reality that one abhors.

The student had a larger challenge than passing tests. He needed to give up the perspective that says he is no good, worthless, if he fails in what he undertakes. His emancipation from this perspective that is determining how he views and interprets his life lies in achieving a more hopeful perspective.

A Liberating Perspective

The Good News is that there is a hopeful perspective—another way of qualifying, or rather, not qualifying. The Good News is that I am exposed before God and it does not matter. Therefore, it need not matter if I am exposed to myself or to others. The Good News is that I am liberated from judgment; so I can relax my defenses and breathe easier. This may seem too easy, too simple—in fact, too good to be true. Can there be such a thing as love with no conditions attached? Is it possible to have a perspective that sees oneself and others, including one's family members, apart from the traditional value judgments of good and bad, winner and loser, superior and inferior, and the like? It is possible if that perspective is based on grace—where qualifying and deserving are not the issues, and judgment, although real, is removed by forgiveness.

People such as my student need to surrender their conditional acceptance of themselves, in which one is of worth only if one

succeeds—and receive instead the unconditional acceptance
that focuses on one's person, not on one's accomplishments.
Theologian Paul Tillich says that nothing greater can happen
to a person than that he or she is forgiven. It is forgiveness that
liberates us from our guilt-oriented perspective so that we can
affirm ourselves as God's beloved. To paraphrase Kierkegaard,
we can endure being transparent before the God who created us,
and *will* to be who we are. The double-mindedness caused by
guilt is overcome when we are reconciled with ourselves.

The problem is that this Good News can remain an abstraction that we know in our heads while we remain in bondage to
bad news in our hearts. It is unapplied in the deeper levels of our
person—symbolized by the heart—because our self-judgment
gets in the way. As one of my counselees said, "I can't stand my
own company. I just hate my double-minded self!" "You are
double-minded, all right," I responded, "but I have good news
for you: you are a forgiven double-minded, and this makes all
the difference in the world." How, then, to see ourselves in this
radically different light?

Since reconciliation with who we are is the only way to become unified within, how can we extend this forgiveness from
God to ourselves—so that the Good News actually becomes
Good News for us? A preacher I heard said it well: "When you
quit prosecuting yourself you will be acquitted." The judge
wants to accept us, not because of the law, but because of grace.
But as our own prosecutors we hammer away on the basis of
law, and of course, on this basis we will pronounce ourselves
guilty. Only mercy can triumph over such judgment (James
2:13). So take a look in the mirror—a good hard look, spare
yourself nothing. Then tell yourself the Good News. "This is
the self that's loved!" Imagine God's arms reaching out from
Christ's cross and embracing you—all of you, your total self.
Now, move into this new perspective and embrace yourself—all
of yourself. If you sense some resistance, it is because your old

perspective based on the law is persisting, and you are still feeling unlovable. By the standards of the law, of course, you are unlovable. But grace has no such standards; it is without conditions; it is unqualified acceptance.

It is easy to confuse acceptance with approval. If we had to wait until God could approve of all of our thoughts, words, motives, and actions before he could accept us, how long would we wait? The Good News is that we do not have to wait! His acceptance does not depend on his approval. He can disapprove of how we behave "inwardly and outwardly" and still accept our person—our self. So go ahead and approve or disapprove of the way you function, for this is the first step in your self-improvement, providing you allow yourself to be accepted in spite of your approval or disapproval.

Since God's love is without conditions and we are accepted as we are, there is no need to deny anything about ourselves—our anger toward our loved ones, our petty irritation or jealousy toward our friends, our defensive dishonesty, or our cowardly fears. Nor is there any need to be defensive. What is there to defend if we are accepted as we are? Nor is there any need to project blame onto others. The best defense is a good offense only when we need a defense. Nor is there any need to punish ourselves—to berate, browbeat, or depress ourselves. These are all ways that we use to make atonement for our guilt. But God himself has made the atonement through Christ. You have all the reason you will ever need to forgive yourself.

Forgiveness draws the curtain on the past. Its guilty hold over us is broken. We not only have permission, we are invited, rather, we are called, to break out of the cycles that bind us to our past, to enter into the new—new experiences, new frontiers, new growth. Though such emancipations may take place only here and there and now and then in our experience, their potential is inherent in every present moment.

The opposite of forgiveness—our residual and unresolved

guilt—binds us to our past. We repeat it—especially those parts of it about which we feel guilty. Freud noted this phenomenon and called it the repetition compulsion. Eric Berne gave it the more colloquial label of "playing old tapes." How do we turn off these tapes so that we can cut a new one? We turn them off by letting forgiveness—grace—influence the way we relate to ourselves. Letting can be described also as ceasing to resist, for the Spirit of God calls us continually to become open—to be receptive to this grace that is all about us. As we respond to his call, we bring closure to our past so that the present moment—each present moment—can be a new beginning, a fresh start free of all the negative circumstances that otherwise would frustrate any change.

Whatever is new—really new—can also be frightening. There are no signposts to reassure us that we have been this way before. We could get lost! We can become so preoccupied with guilt, with being down on ourselves, with misery of one form or another, that becoming free of these stresses may cause us to panic. Unfilled space, like unfilled time, terrifies. What will take its place? The answer depends on our identity. Confusion over our identity, however, is another cause—or form—of double-mindedness.

5

To Whom Are You Married?

The word identity has taken on a new meaning in recent years. So and so, we say, is having an identity crisis, or he or she has no identity. We do not mean, of course, that such persons are suffering from amnesia, but that they are confused about who they are, even though their memory is intact. The very fact that we can speak of knowing or not knowing who we are reveals the complexity of human nature. Something can go amiss between my subjective I and my objective me so that confusion exists between them.

This confusion over our identity is another cause of double-mindedness. The self-direction that characterizes single-mindedness depends upon the clarity of our intentions. Paradoxically, the confusion over our identity is also caused by double-mindedness. So double-mindedness is a hindrance to resolving our identity confusion, and our identity confusion is a hindrance to overcoming our double-mindedness. As is often the case when confusion reigns, we easily become immobilized, since we cannot see clearly enough in any direction to move with confidence.

The synonym that I choose to use for identity is commitment. Our identity is formed by our loyalties, our allegiances, which provide a focus for our perspective. Commitment is an influence for unity, but confusion is divisive. Commitment also has transcendent implications. One is devoted to something or someone beyond—larger than—oneself. In religious language, this devotion is ultimately to the Creator and is expressed through worship. Our identity, then, is shaped by the nature of our commitment—the character of the god to whom we give our allegiance.

The Desire to Possess God

The word *my* is a possessive pronoun. Its use indicates that the object in question is closely connected with oneself. This connection may be an intimate and caring relationship; it may also be a possessive relationship. There is a definite, but at times subtle, difference between these two. So the words *my husband, my wife, my child, my friend* may have either implication. So also the words my God.

As an exclamation, the words *my God* may come almost involuntarily when we are confronted with some shocking or painful sensation or insight. These sudden awarenesses are frequently negative in character, or even horrible. Jesus used these words in his agony on the cross. "My God—why!" In saying "My God," we are spontaneously, and perhaps even unconsciously, calling on the deity for some kind of support as our sensibilities are being invaded by data too horrendous to process—paradoxically, a cry of disbelief when confronted by knowledge too shocking to believe. I discover myself saying "Lord Jesus" in such circumstances. These words may also constitute a cry of impotency when confronted by events beyond our control. What we may actually be saying is "My God—help!"

The words *my God* may also indicate our desire to possess God. A possessive relationship is one in which one of the participants controls, or would like to control, the other. People may use this sort of relationship with their deity as a way of controlling other people. "My Jesus" they say, "would not talk [act, feel] that way!" This coercive way of using the deity is shown also in the familiar formula: If God wanted us to do this or that [say, smoke], he would have created us in this or that way [say, with chimneys]. Since no finite human being can know so assuredly the mind of God, we are in reality informing God of what we think should be in his mind.

This "possessed" God is easily manipulated, since he exists only in the realm of our fantasy. He is often sentimentalized, being identified with what "feels right" to us. Like all fantasy characters, this God is manipulated by our desires and interests.

In my counseling, I have observed this kind of fantasizing when people need to justify their questionable behavior. Although she went through the motions of seeking marriage counseling, Mary was resistant to being reconciled with her husband. She defended her reluctance by saying she thought it was too late. The fact was that she had a lover. Yet Mary was a religious person. I was curious, therefore, about how she evaluated her behavior religiously, since to me she seemed closed-minded. So I began by asking her if she prayed about the problem. Without hesitation she answered, "I talk to my God every day." Although I knew I was biased, I still wanted to say, "What about *the* God, Mary, not just *your* God." Had I pursued this I would have "invaded her space." I was aware also that we all struggle with the temptation to subjectivize God.

In ways symbolized by the subtle change in emphasis from my God to my God, we human beings try to cross the abyss that separates us as creatures from the Creator in order to usurp to some extent God's place. J. B. Phillips emphasized this danger in his book, *Your God Is Too Small*. Another way of describing this reduction of God is "God in a box." Such a God has no identity apart from our possessiveness, as is the case with our other fantasy characters or even with some people who permit themselves to be possessed or controlled by another. God then becomes our own creation, fashioned by our mind to give sanction to our desires. Instead of our being created in God's image, God has been created in ours.

If we find it difficult to "let God be God" because of our own need to be in control, because of this same need, we will find it difficult also to relate to other people. Some persons who come to a counselor—supposedly for counseling—do not want to accept the other as a counselor. They maintain control by questioning the counselor's method or by resisting his or her insights without giving them serious consideration. Manifesting this kind of resistance is different from behaving as a responsible person who retains responsibility for his or her own problems, solutions, and growth. The resister chooses to stay outside the relationship rather than become involved and possibly lose control. The attitude displayed in this resistance is symbolic of how some people interpret life as a whole; they screen it before it touches them so that they are not exposed to anything that would in any way threaten them. They prejudge so they will not experience. Nothing new, therefore, can enter their consciousness. Forging the chains that bind them to the old, they prevent their own opportunities—opportunities that the Spirit might use to effect the changes needed in their lives for growth.

Be Still and Know

An opposite approach to this defensive stance is contained in the words of Psalm 46. "Be still and know that I am God." Be *still,* that is, be *secure* in knowing that God is God. I include these words in my daily meditation. Actually I find them to be quite a relief. It is good to realize that I am really not God—that I am not alone. Focusing on these words helps me to become still as I center myself, get my perspective. I am *under* God and not *as* God. Within this perspective, I regain my capacity for trust. I do not need frenetically to fill all the empty spaces in order to guard against the unknown and unforeseen. "Be still" means also to be open, for how else can I be receptive to what God intends for me, or even be surprised by it. The unknown does not have to be frightening when I know that He is God.

"Know that *I* am God." The I is the unpossessed God. He is as the theologian Karl Barth says, the Wholly Other. Although he is the Wholly Other, he has given himself wholly to us. We see this balance in the similar words of the First Commandment, "*I* am the Lord *thy* God." He is unpossessed, but he is also my God. Martin Luther received much comfort from this commandment. He was a man of great emotional and intellectual fluctuation, and found his source of stabilization in the God who had committed Himself to him. Like some others, Luther had his bouts with depression. There were times when the burden of his responsibilities grew too heavy, and it seemed that nothing he did was right. Then the words of this commandment would come to his mind and he would know once again that God was not only alive and well but also caring for him.

"I am the Lord thy God. Thou shalt have no other gods beside me." Although in our so-called civilized societies we no longer make gods out of wood and stone, our penchant for idolatry, as Paul Tillich has emphasized, remains the same. Our possessed and fantasy gods are good examples of civilized idolatry. It is the God beyond these Gods, says Tillich, who is "the Lord our God," and when these possessed and fantasy gods collapse under the weight of reality, "the God beyond God" will reveal himself.

Because of our tendency to reduce God to the image of our desires, we need a source beyond our subjective perceptions for our understanding of God. The Bible is such a source, providing us with a rich tradition about the nature and purposes of God. It can sustain us when our subjective perceptions go awry in the same way as it did Luther. Although it is called the Word of God, the Bible is more than words. The Word actually is a historical event or a series of historical events. Jesus, for example, is called the Living Word in that he revealed the God beyond God in the events of his life, death, and resurrection. The Bible is also the tradition of a community of faith created around these events. While the Bible is inseparable from this historical evolving of the Old and New Covenants, it is also inseparable from the community of faith that continues as an ongoing witness to these events. This community is the larger context within which the Bible functions as the Word of God.

It was this community of faith that sustained Kathryn Koob for 444 days as an American held as a hostage in Iran, even though she was isolated in a tiny bedroom with the curtains closed. In her solitude, the memories of that community filled her mind—the hymns, the psalms, the stories of the Bible. Where did these words and mental pictures come from? "Now I realize," she says, "that I was given a vast treasure of worship and devotional materials from my earliest childhood days. And I am so grateful for it." After five months she was permitted a roommate, fellow hostage Ann Swift. Soon the two of them began having their devotional times together and in that small "community of faith" a deep friendship developed. Listen to how Kathryn Koob reflects on that harrowing experience.

Our captivity was long and difficult. But I found my days filled with the spirit and power of the Lord. Those 444 days became a time of spiritual growth because I had had a lifetime of preparation for what I faced in Tehran. From the first time my hands were folded and I was taught to say "Amen" by my parents, I was guided by them and by grandparents, god-parents, and fellow members of the family of Christians. The faith they had shared with me sustained me, by God's grace, when the mobs in the streets by the embassy were screaming, "Death! Death!" Because of what I had been given, I knew I was safe in the love of our Lord.[5]

Of course, even in the context of the community of faith, the Bible is not a purely external input into our understanding of God, since it must be interpreted. In fact, it is this highly subjective task of interpreting that has contributed to the many divisions in Christendom. Yet there is still something objectively present to be interpreted. In this sense the Bible as the Word of God is like all other data that come to us through our senses. In interpreting its meaning we run the risk of subjective distortion.

Yet, even here, we have help from external sources. The many scientific studies of the Bible—although not spared the subjective coloration of scholars who are also divided—provide an outside assist to our interpretive function.

Still, we do not want only to apologize for the subjective input into our understanding. In the last analysis, as Kierkegaard has said, "subjectivity is truth," that is, it is truth for *me*. If the Bible is not simply a book but the Word of God through which the Spirit of God speaks to my spirit, there is of necessity a core of subjectivity to my understanding of the Word. I can share this understanding with others, and they may profit from it. But ultimately for this to happen, it must also become *their* understanding. Job stated the matter well as he reflected on the change that occurred in his understanding after his encounter with God. "I had heard of thee by the hearing of the ear, but now my eye sees thee" (Job 42:5).

To Whom Is One Married?

Another way to put the identity question, Who is your God? is, To whom are you married? This question is also related to the Bible, in that in both the Old and New Testaments one's relationship to God, both as an individual and as a member of a community of faith, is described as a marriage. Our relationships—or the contemporary term, systems—are a heavy influence on us either in establishing our identity or in confusing it. For example, a particular marriage can be a possessive invasion of space on the part of one or both partners that actually obstructs the formation of a true marriage. It is interesting to note the differences in behavior among persons who have lost a mate through death. Normally the grief is overwhelming, and it takes a year or two before one can return to living with some degree of normalcy. Some seem never to return; in effect, they died with their mate. The degree of dependency was so great that they lacked sufficient identity alone even to want to survive.

But some seem to come to life after the death. I know of an elderly widow who is amazing all of her friends by the change in her personality. During her marriage she was reserved and even withdrawn, but after her husband's death she became exuberant. Participating actively in groups in which heretofore she was passive, she displayed an obvious talent for leadership. She gave all the appearances of being emancipated. She *was* emancipated—from a marriage in which she felt not only inhibited but imprisoned. During her marriage her husband referred to her as "my wife," and she was indeed his wife—owned, controlled, and shaped into the image he desired. Yet he was married only to this image, not to a person, certainly not to the person of his wife.

But theirs was a caricature of marriage, obviously not the sort of marriage that is analogous to our relationship with God. Ben Patterson, writing in the *Wittenburg Door*, compares the anxiety one may have in contemplating what faith in God means for one's life to the anxiety he experienced prior to his marriage. "About a month before our marriage, I went through a terrible panic. Never before had so many girls looked so interesting to me. That was because I had finally realized that to say 'yes' to the girl who finally became my wife, would mean to say 'no' to millions of others! That is exactly what I ended up doing at my wedding ceremony."[6] When one becomes married to the person of another, one is provided a powerful identity focus, as Patterson so clearly revealed.

Based on this understanding of marriage as commitment, adultery is an act of identity confusion. The same is true with our marriage to God. Appalled by the way in which Christians were being caught up in the ways of the world, James, in the spirit of the Old Testament prophets, charged them with adultery. "Unfaithful creatures [literally adulterers]! Do you not know that friendship with the world is enmity with God?" (James 4:4). When one is married one makes an either-or choice. Usually we associate an either-or stance with rigidity, in contrast to a both-and approach in which there is greater flexibility as well as wisdom. But in marriage a both-and approach is a compromise of one's identity—a symptom of the double mind. In John's Gospel, Christians are described as being in the world but not of it. We live in an environment alien to our marriage. We live continuously with this tension—an identity tension. It is significant that James, in describing the either-or of friendship with God or the world, calls friendship with the world adultery. Marriage is essentially a friendship, but a particular—a unique—kind of friendship. Somebody has defined it as friendship plus sex. Although we can interpret this in various ways, I interpret it to mean a friendship that is uniquely and intimately committed. There is a covenant in marriage that affirms our identity.

The prophet Elijah described well the disintegrating effects of double-mindedness in our commitment when he asked the people supposedly committed to the Lord but enticed into the Baal worship of their neighbors, " 'How long will you go limping with two different opinions? If the Lord is God, follow him; but if Baal, then follow him.' And the people did not answer him a word" (1 Kings 18:21). They did not answer him a word because they knew he was right, but they were not ready to act on his either-or exhortation and therefore would continue to limp.

Marriage is a commitment. Ben Patterson made this commitment, he said, at his wedding ceremony. In our marriage to God, the equivalent of the wedding ceremony is baptism, the rite in which we are joined to, united with, covenanted to God. Unless you were baptized after your infancy, you probably cannot recall this momentous day in your life, so young were you when covenanted. Yet you know it happened. The community of faith into which you were covenanted as God's spouse is the witness. Our baptism is not only the rite of our commitment to God but also—

and primarily so—of God's commitment to us. Realizing this can make the difference at critical moments of identity crisis. A former counselee shared with me what has stuck in her memory from our counseling days. "It was when you said, 'Remember your are baptized—you know who you are.' This gave me the courage to face an ordeal from which I would much rather have run." When you become aware at any particular moment that "God is faithful," you will know more clearly who you are—and to whom you are committed.

6

Single-Mindedness Through Commitment

For James, God's competitor for our either-or devotion is the world. By the world he is not referring, of course, to our planet as such, but to the value system associated with human society that is opposed to that of the Kingdom of God. Western society is itself characterized by competition and has a penchant on this basis for dividing people into winners and losers. What is at stake is one's worth as a person. Although as God's spouse we are not of the world, we are still in it and therefore susceptible to the lure of the competitive rat race for determining our worth, in essence our identity.

The Seductive World

In the winter I run on an indoor track that is often crowded. On one occasion, there were only three of us, but others eventually arrived. In the locker room afterward I commented to the original two about the emptiness of the track. "I was glad when others came," said one. "I like company—I enjoy it more then." "I was glad also," said the other, "but I liked the competition—I run better then." It struck me that these divergent reactions to the presence of others reflected the two most commonly held attitudes toward people.

Competition is built in to our cultural mystique in our idealization of American "rugged individualism." Although there is something heroic about a person who is sufficient in him or herself and who stands apart from others as an independent spirit, were many to follow this model, the sense of cooperative endeavor and interdependency needed for caring community living would soon dissipate. In this perspective, rugged individualism is a flawed ideal and a faulty model. As cultural analyst Philip Slater has observed, our revolutions and rebellions are really revivals; so "Do your own thing" is a revival of rugged individualism.

A corollary to such individualism is that one seeks first one's own fulfillment. The human potential movement that spawned this search for fulfillment has done much to emancipate people from crippling dependencies in their relationships. Yet, an individualism that in turn cripples community living is really no answer to such dependency. Rather, it looks more like the world that James says is opposed to God, for if one seeks first one's own fulfillment how can one also "seek first his [God's] kingdom" (Matt. 6:33)?

The problem with old and new forms of individualism is that the mutuality that makes for community living, including marriage and family, is de-emphasized. Each of us is not only a giver but also a receiver, and not only a receiver but also a giver. The answer to crippling dependency is the mutuality of interdependence. I know people who, bitten by the world's adulation of independence, insist in being only givers. In fact, the profession to which I belong and whose candidates I teach is a prime example of this tendency. The clergy are by profession ministers. They are the ones who are called to serve others. This makes it difficult for them to also be receivers. As preachers they are supposed to have the answers. How then can they ask the questions? Particularly of the people to whom they minister? The role is so conditioning that clergy find it difficult to receive even from their own professional brothers and sisters, or even from other professionals. Their identity is threatened should they acknowledge their own need to receive. This kind of caricature of the ministry is a prime cause for professional and personal burnout. The imbalance or lack of mutuality ultimately has its consequences.

Actually, those who insist on being only givers are, ironically, insisting on being only receivers. The giver is on top in the world's values. He or she is a winner. Hence, the giver receives all of the ego satisfaction in the transaction, leaving the receiver with none. Those who are only receivers, either in their relationships or in their role in the community, have little self-esteem. It is no mystery then that they sometimes feel so little gratitude to the givers, but may instead feel antipathy. If as Jesus said, "It is more blessed to give than to receive" (Acts 20:35), the givers have "hogged" the blessing—leaving the receivers not only without the blessing but with the identity, loser.

But giving does not have to close the door to one's receiving. In fact, giving can open this door if our commitment is to God and not to the world. In the Sermon on the Mount, Jesus described how it works.

Give, and it will be given to you; good measure, pressed down, shaken together, running over, will be put into your lap. For the measure you give will be the measure you get back. (Luke 6:38).

In my teaching of pastoral counseling, we use our advanced students as teaching assistants. Ostensibly it is the advanced students who are the givers—of their experience, knowledge, wisdom. And they do give. But I have repeatedly noticed that the advanced students are also the receivers. And the more they put into their giving, the more they receive. Over and over again these teaching assistants say, "I've learned so much in this experience—probably more than the students I've supervised."

Some enterprising entrepreneurs openly exploit the biblical origin of this principle of receiving through giving and use it to increase profits. While their attitude may not prevent the principle from "working," it does cause a problem when it "works." What does one do with the profits?—with the "good measure, pressed down, shaken together, running over, [that] will be put into your lap"? How much can one lap hold? We are now in an identity crisis. The world has a ready answer—get another lap, and another and another. In other words, keep it! But this is far different from the biblical answer.

This same attitude is revealed in the farmer in Jesus' parable who had a bumper crop. "What shall I do," he asked, "for I have nowhere to store my crops?" Being a man of the world he came up with the familiar answer. "I will do this: I will pull down my barns, and build larger ones; and there I will store all my grain and my goods" (Luke 12:17–18). "Build bigger barns" could be the watchword for our gross national product mentality. One must show growth and therefore have more storage space. Jesus' judgment on the farmer was not that he was a bad person, but that he was a fool. He had devoted himself to the world's value system and ultimately it would "sell him short." He missed out on the joy he could have received in distributing his surplus to those in need.

In contrast to the foolishness of the farmer in building bigger barns to store his surplus is the wisdom in the story of the manna from heaven that the people of the Old Covenant received while traveling through the wilderness (Exod. 16:14–21). Manna was a breadlike substance that the people discovered covering the ground when they were hungry. Seeing it as bread that the Lord had given to them, Moses directed the people to gather as much as they needed for the day, but no more. Those who had a hard time restraining themselves discovered that the surplus they had gathered rotted by the following morning.

The parable of the farmer in the New Testament and the story of the manna in the Old Testament teach a radically different life-style from that of the world. E. F. Schumacher, a Christian as well as an economist, wrote his book, *Small Is*

Beautiful, to protest the world's obsession with bigger barns. Jesus told the parable of the farmer when he was asked to mediate an inheritance dispute between two brothers. "A man's life," he said, "does not consist in the abundance of his possessions." The appeal of the world implies that it does.

I am amazed at how the systems of our society, our cultural assumptions, our money and other possessions control us and make our decisions. People buy more things—property, cars, cabins, boats—and then feel obligated to devote their time and energy to them. Our possessions actually possess *us!* Weighed down by their care, we lose the freedom of those who "travel lightly." Or look at the manner in which the insurance system influences our endeavors. Experiments in home care for the ill and the elderly, for example, are curtailed because medical insurance is confined primarily to health care institutions. Our pension plans, including social security, determine whether we can or cannot work in our later years. Or do they? Is it not rather our assumption that the money we have coming to us should determine how we live? For would we not be fools if we did not collect our money, even if this means that we must alter our lifestyle to get it? Or are we really fools to let money determine the way we live? We assume a necessity in these matters that is really not so. The options to the system have remained largely undeveloped or even unexplored because our materialistic assumptions lead to self-imposed limits.

Closely associated with the world's fascination with bigness and its domination by money is its preoccupation with packaging—or as it is more commonly called, image building. Everything has to look good. Our purchases must be packaged. Philip Slater says that to carry something we have purchased down the street unwrapped would seem obscene—as though we ourselves were naked. Politicians are obsessed with taking their political pulse in the latest poll to see how they are being received; if the indications are negative, the experts are called in to devise ways of "improving the image." How does it look? How do we look? The merchant also appeals to the image. What impression will this suit—dress—outfit—automobile—create on others? Even those who rebelled against the pressures of fashion in the counterculture days used clothing—old, sloppy, simple, whatever— to project an image. All of this packaging, image building, clothing, and style preoccupation bypasses, in fact, deliberately avoids, the basic question of who we are—transparent and unadorned.

Question All Authority

We have talked about what undermines community living; now it is time to talk about what creates and supports it. If we were to list the values and attitudes opposite to those of our competitive culture we would be off to a good start. Cooperation instead of competition, compassion instead of aggression, generosity instead of greed (bigger barns)—these are the qualities that foster community.

If there is one quality that is fundamental to the others, it is gratitude. Gratitude begets the generosity that reaches out to others in compassionate support. Saint Paul points to the legitimate basis for this gratitude when he asks the rhetorical question, "What have you that you did not receive?" (1 Cor. 4:7). So-called self-made persons fail to realize the gifts they have been given. At a conference on the Christian life, there was a discussion about the oppression of the poor. A man whom I know to be a dedicated Christian took exception to the discussion. "If you want to talk about the poor in the Third World, I will agree that they are oppressed, but I believe in our own country the poor have no excuse. Look at the opportunities here in America. I myself came from a poor family and I worked as a kid to help support it. I went to night school while I was supporting a wife and two children until I finally got my high school diploma— and then years later my college degree. I pulled myself up by my own bootstraps—and I'm not going to feel sorry for people who are too lazy to do the same."

This man, of course, had a point. There are people who do not take advantage of their opportunities and who even exploit those who try to help them. But what he could not see was what his judging of these people was doing to himself. Because he had "made it" in our society by the sweat of his brow, he had ceased to be grateful. He no longer recognized the advantages that he had in our society—a white skin, a healthy body, a good physical appearance, an intelligent mind, caring parents, a belief in himself as well as in God, a supportive wife and an extended family in the congregation, and for his day, the advantage of being a male. Yet he believes he pulled himself up by his own bootstraps! His is a confused identity: on the one hand, his bootstrap attitude belongs to the world, and on the other, his commitment to God is on the basis of grace. His divided identity came to the fore in his attitude to the poor.

"What have you that you have not received?" If he accepts Paul's question as legitimate, then he must deal with Paul's conclusion. "If then you received it, why do you boast as if it were not a gift?" (1 Cor. 4:7). If he could see his identity confusion in his boasting and judging, and reaffirm himself in his covenant of grace, he would receive another gift—a grateful heart. From this gift comes the generosity of spirit that characterizes those who know that in every way they are receivers— recipients of grace.

How could one as devoted to God as this man have become also an advocate of the opposing value system of the world? James would say he was seduced. Using language related to seduction he writes, "Each person is tempted when he is lured and enticed by his own desire" (James 1:14). In other words, we have within us a divided loyalty—the double mind. Identity confusion occurs when the unacknowledged mind, by the age-old tricks of luring and enticing, moves us to compromise in our commitment. Seduced by the ego satisfaction that comes from boasting—I worked hard for what I have and therefore deserve it—this man at that point became a friend of the world. Another way of putting it is that he became acculturated in his socio-political-economic views. We encounter this kind of acculturation quite frequently when Christians confuse a nationalism—in our case, Americanism—with devotion to the Kingdom of God, and an economic system—in our case, the free enterprise system—with Christianity.

I saw a T-shirt recently that I want to purchase. It has the words Question All Authority on the front. To maintain our identity as the people of God I believe this is precisely what we must do. We are continually lured into accepting as authority that which is not our authority. These seductions begin with "What will people—the neighbors, the relatives, the public—think?" and grow to include whatever is currently accepted as patriotic, square, successful, loyal to the company, pious, free, bold, "swinging," or well done. We need to question all rules and assumptions—the way "everybody (or at least the people with whom we want to identify) does it" or assumes it has to be done. Otherwise an uncritical acceptance of these authorities can become the straitjacket on our potential for development as persons. We need an individualism that is identified with integrity rather than independence. If the latter is associated with American rugged individualism, the former is associated with the priesthood of every beliver. Although we live in the world—participants in human culture and involved in human institutions—we are not of the world; our ultimate authority is not in these human creations.

A veteran pastor whom I regard highly told me that in his earlier days in the ministry he was preoccupied with trying to please the people of his church, until, in utter fatigue and confusion, he decided he would focus instead on pleasing God and let God worry about pleasing the people. This decision emancipated him to be who he was.

But there is a risk, of course, in not being of the world. Who wants to be thought of as stupid—to "be taken advantage of" or to "lose out" or "miss out" on cultural rewards? Along with others, we desire the acclaim that goes to "winners." Since we depend on cultural values to determine who is a winner, and *ipso facto*, a loser, we find ourselves in a kind of cultural solipsism. This is the real stupidity. Who gave to our cultural values this authority? They remain authoritative simply because they are assumed rather than evaluated. In reckoning with this tension of *in* but not *of*, Kierkegaard advises the Christian, whom he calls the lover, to take the risk (in loving) of being exploited, defrauded, or rejected—to be God's fool. This is a different kind of fool from the farmer who built bigger barns. God's fools are the only wise ones among us, because they see the folly in the so-called wisdom of the world. As Saint Paul said, "If any one among you thinks that he is wise in this age, let him become a fool that he may become wise. For the wisdom of this world is folly with God" (1 Cor. 3:18–19). By the same token, "the word of the cross is folly to those who are perishing" (2 Cor. 1:18). For, as Jesus said, "The sons of this world are wiser in their own generation than the sons of light" (Luke 16:8).

Through Complexity to Commitment

Questioning all authority is not an end in itself. Unfortunately, it becomes this way for some people. They forever question but never take a stand—commit themselves. They are no better off than those who go along without questioning. Questioning is necessary because of the complexity situations take on when one is in the world but not of it. To have a single mind, however, it is necessary to decide. Oliver Wendell Holmes said, "I do not give a fig for the simplicity this side of complexity, but I would give my life for the simplicity on the other side of complexity." There is a remarkable simplicity to decision once we have worked through to clarity what it is we want.

The parable of the pearl of great price illustrates this simplicity. Considered by the ancients as the most precious and valued of gems, the pearl in this parable is symbolic of the Kingdom of Heaven. A pearl merchant discovered this most valuable of pearls. Knowing what he wanted, his course was clear. He sold everything he had to raise the money to buy the pearl (Matt. 13:45-46). Such is the determination of a unified mind.

So we come to the question, What do you really want? In determining this, you are approaching the essence of freedom. Bring your double-mindedness out into the open. Get it out of the "game" stage so that you know what is going on. When you do, you may see that you want what you have always acknowledged you wanted, but you may also have a desire, subtle and even insidious, for its opposite. Here, then, is your divided loyalty—the source of your temptation. When you pray, "Lead us not into temptation," you are reflecting your trust in God to protect you from your own vulnerability. We know *who* we are from knowing *whose* we are.

At about the same time Eric Berne published *Transactional Analysis,* in which he developed his parent-adult-child understanding of the human personality, W. Hugh Missildine published *Your Inner Child of the Past,* with a different emphasis in a similar format. For Missildine, one becomes an adult when one becomes the parent of one's inner child. This marks a transition from internalizing one's parents to developing one's own parent. In Missildine's imagery, there is an interesting correspondence with the familiar biblical description of marriage. "Therefore a man leaves his father and his mother and cleaves to his wife, and they become one flesh" (Gen. 2:24).

Leaving father and mother is a psychological prerequisite not only for cleaving to one's mate but, in a broader sense, for being an adult, whether married or single. In becoming our own parent of our inner child of the past, we transcend, or mature out of, the natural struggles between resistance (or rebellion) and conformity that perpetuate our double-mindedness. This makes possible an internal unity—now and then—amidst the diversity of parent and child. Our commitment then is from within and our behavior is a reflection of it. It is this commitment that enables us to resolve our inner division. Such resolutions occur moment by moment and are renewals, or even celebrations, of our commitment.

7

Arbitrary Limitation Versus Accepting Limits

People who assume undue authority or domination are sometimes accused of "playing God." Although we understand what is meant by "playing God," the term is a misnomer. Such people are not playing God but are playing at being God. And in fact they are not playing at all; rather, they are taking themselves very seriously.

Playing God

Playing God is not confined to a few arrogant sorts who refuse to acknowledge their fallibility. On the contrary, playing God is the essence of what it is to be a sinner. Our dissatisfaction with being creatures leads us at times to want to be our own God. This human envy of the deity focuses on our limits; we are often painfully aware of them. The Creator, in contrast, is unlimited save for such limits as are self-imposed.

In the insatiability of our egos we want it all; we resist all limits to what we can acquire. It seems we just can't get enough if there is still some to get—or if others have more. Even those who seem to have much of everything can be obsessed with getting more. Poet Phyllis McGinley wrote, "Give the rich to please them, riches."[7] It will not please them for long if there is more out there to get. This obsession with more robs us of any satisfaction with what we have.

The limits against which we chafe are not confined to money and material possessions. The current emphasis on "fulfilling our potential" and "meeting our needs" ties in easily with this tendency. Pioneer psychologist William James estimated that we humans fulfill only ten percent of our potential as persons, and human potentialist Herbert Otto says it is only five percent. The desire for self-improvement can be a healthy attribute and even a necessary stimulus for change. There is a difference, however, between having a vision for our life and being driven to achieve an ever-elusive goal. It is one thing to "hitch one's wagon to a star"; it is another to be desperately driven to escape the judgment of not reaching that star. In our contemporary preoccupation with fulfillment, we have, as Daniel Yankelovich says, "an imperative to fill all our needs . . . a determination to consume every plate on the smorgasbord of human experience."[8] This compulsion is no different from less sophisticated ones in its ability to make us miserable.

The impossibility of the quest rests on a subtle confusion of needs with desires. A need is something that is necessary, something we cannot do without and still survive. We need food, for example, and protection from the elements. Children need a caring relationship. We desire a lot more than we need—and this is as it should be. But we can survive—as many have demonstrated—with severe privations. A counselor whom I know tends to stop a counselee when he or she says, "I need," and if the matter is really a desire, he has the person say, "I want." Obviously, when wants are considered needs, there is no limit to our needs.

Adding to the Limits We Chafe Under

Ironically, we humans add to the very limits that we resist. Not all self-imposed limits, however, are self-defeating. When I commit myself to a task or to a person, I voluntarily limit my options. As a married person, for example, I limit my options with other women. I may be aesthetically and sexually attracted to this or that woman, but I accept the limits in my pursuance of this attraction. I allow myself to enjoy the attraction without chafing unduly at the limits I have imposed on it. When we make decisions, we limit our choices. On the other hand, if we make no decisions we ultimately lose all choices. As Yankelovich has discerned, people who want to "enlarge their choices" by "seeking to keep all options open" actually "diminish them."[9]

Many of our self-imposed limitations, however, are arbitrary and destructive. When such is the case, we increase our limits for the protection of the same ego that cannot get enough—an example of the contradictions that grow out of our double-mindedness. This ego wants everything but does not want to fail at anything. Above all else it fears humiliation. Since it will "go around Robinson's barn" to avoid a negative judgment, it cannot afford any risks that might cause it to be stigmatized by our competitive comparativeness as weird or different or loser.

For the protection of our egos, we adopt the myths that support the inertia of the status quo. These protective assumptions provide the justification we want for adding to the limits that we also resist. We become wedded to old ways of doing things; we assume there are no other options and find it comforting to have none. We do not scrutinize what we are used to. We assume we have more control over what we are familiar with, and we may overscrutinize new ways that seem to threaten this control. Satir calls this irrational holding on to the old "mental retardation." In a lecture she gave as an example the practice she grew up with in her rural community of cutting roast beef so that it could be cooked in two pans. It was thought that this was the only right way to do it. What everybody had forgotten was that grandma started the practice because she did not have one pan that was big enough. It is such "jungle stories in our attic," she said, that kill off our curiosity. What we are accustomed to provides us with what Karen Horney calls the security of the familiar. We feel less threatened when we can recognize some familiar landmark.

Holding Fast to the Status Quo

Both the ego's desire to be unlimited and its need for protective limits interfere with changing our old ways. It is difficult to make a decision to change these ways; it is even more difficult to implement this decision and more difficult still to perpetuate the change. The challenge is analogous to the experience of losing weight. When overweight people deal with their double-mindedness and decide to lose weight, they have reached their initial milestone. The strength of that decision, however, is tested by the rigors of dieting that follow it. If the weight is lost, they reach the second milestone—keeping the weight off. But this has no terminus—no milestone at which one can arrive, no ending after which one can relax—and therefore is the most difficult.

There are risks in making changes in our life—whether by accepting our limits or by challenging them—and therefore we may be double-minded about such changes. The religious term for change is repentance, meaning literally "a change of mind." A church secretary told me her concern about a very active member of her church who is known for never changing his mind on anything. Naturally, he is a difficult person to relate to. But of even more concern, how has he been able to avoid repentance in a Christian community? This is like being afraid to enter the water when you are on the swimming team.

Yet, this church member is not that far removed from many of us. Do you find it hard to accept limits on what you can do—to make choices? Or would you like, instead, to have it all? It is thus we destine ourselves to frustration, and we churn in our innards because we are not achieving all that we desire.

I like to garden; it is really my hobby. But I have a hard time keeping it a hobby. I tell myself that when my gardening becomes work, I will quit. But of late, I am finding it more difficult to draw the line. Yesterday, I became increasingly frustrated after spending a great part of the day in my garden because I kept seeing more to do than I could get done. I realized that my completion compulsion was getting to me; my garden was becoming my obsession rather than my hobby. So I decided—once again—to accept something less than I desired and to lose a few battles to the weeds and the bugs.

When our drivenness to achieve meets obstacles—like insects, drought, and weeds—we experience the familiar stress of frustration. It is a miserable state of mind, best described as "batting one's head against the wall." If we could relieve it by screaming in panic, or shouting in rage, or crying in despair, we might feel better. But our surroundings may not reinforce us for such explosions. Therefore, many of us instead take it out on our bodies and develop potentially disabling ailments.

In frustration, our focus is always on what is not yet—what is lacking. Frustration is different from depression in that one is still actively engaged in the struggle, but with a minimum of accomplishment and a maximum of exasperation. As with depression, however, in our frustration we have little balance in our view of what we have and where we are. We give little attention to what is going well and much attention to what is going badly. For this reason, Albert Ellis maintains that the way we think affects the way we feel. Novelist Toni Morrison expresses the same view when she says of one of her characters,"He wouldn't know what to feel until he knew what to think."[10] Behind our faulty thinking, says Ellis, is an irrational belief system. We uncritically assume the value judgments of our culture. For example, our lives may be directed by the belief (or rule) that one can take little joy from the good things one has, so long as there are also bad things or things we do not yet have to occupy our attention. The irrationality of a competitive individualism in which limits are viewed either as personal failures or personal affronts seems to elude us. Yet, limits are the inevitable lot of creatures, and each individual is balanced by other individuals in the variety of gifts and shortcomings that constitute community interdependence. So we need to get beyond the rules and beliefs we have learned that keep us from growing, from changing.

If we are limited, then we need to accept—and to make—limiting choices. If we irrationally resist any limits, we can lose it all. Those who try to carry too much may drop everything. A man as wise as Norman Cousins had to learn his lesson the hard way. Faced with one lecture tour after another with very little time to relax in between, he wanted badly to cancel his engagements in January, 1981. But his associate reminded him that the tour was already composed of postponed and deferred dates. "You've just got to do it," she said. "You couldn't get out of this thing unless you had a heart attack or something like that."

Three days later his body cooperated. He had a very severe heart attack, and not only the January engagements, but all engagements were canceled. Reflecting on this turn of events, Cousins said, "If there's something you really don't want to do and you want out of it, your body gives you that out." Ironically, in not accepting his limits, he added another one. He could have canceled his January trip and taken the consequences. He listened to his associate, however, and concluded that he could not do this. "My body, which had been listening to this," he said, "furnished a perfect excuse."[11] And now he has even more serious consequences than had he challenged the pressure against canceling without awaiting "the perfect excuse."

As the Cousins incident illustrates, the limits we arbitrarily impose on ourselves, supposedly to protect our self-image, are actually in the service of death, literally as well as symbolically. One day while I was shopping, a woman approached me saying she recognized me as the one who had introduced Father John Powell at a recent gathering. "I want to tell you what happened to me as a result of that conference," she said.

I took my mother with me—our relationship has not been good. I hoped it might help both of us to go. When Father Powell talked about telling our families and friends that we love them, I inwardly argued with him. This was something I said I couldn't do. But he knocked down every one of my arguments. So at my first opportunity, I decided to do it. I took my mother in my arms and told her I loved her. She tensed a bit but she liked it—and that marked the beginning of a whole new relationship. I've been praying for years for this to happen. Now it's spreading even to my brothers and sisters!

I felt about as good as she did as I caught the joy in her voice.

Later, my joy was tempered by some sober reflection. She had been praying for years for this to happen. What had prevented her from telling her mother she loved her during all of this time? It obviously had seemed such an impossible approach that she did not consider it. Her resistance was a protective limitation. She probably used "This sort of thing wouldn't work in our family" or some other such arbitrary dismissal. The good point is that she finally did it. The Powell address might also have influenced her mother to be able to receive her daughter's gesture. The story, however, has its shadow in other stories of what-might-have-been in the lives of so many people.

Sometimes we project these limits onto other people. "My spouse (parents, children, siblings, friends, co-workers) will not cooperate!" One of the woman's arguments with Powell, for example, was that her mother would react negatively to an embrace. Yet she had not tested out this assumption. Those with whom we live or associate are also conditioned by their environment, resisting what they are not accustomed to, even though they may complain about the way things are. So when you suggest a change, they may not support you. If you are shaky already about your decision, this lack of support may unsettle you because it will activate, as well as exacerbate, whatever double-mindedness you have.

We are more dependent on the support of others than we may like to think. Perhaps you are fortunate enought to have had people who encouraged you to make changes and take risks. There are many people who frankly admit that without such encouragement from a spouse or parent or teacher or friend, they might have stayed mired in the status quo. If we were together now in conversation, I would offer you my support because I would want to see you break through these arbitrary limitations to be the person you really are. So let me give it to you even so. (If it means so much to receive support, also think how much it may mean for you to give it.) Yet, even with such encouragement, the involvement has to come from your own determination. Even though some among your associates may be encouraging, others may not. There is an inertia in the status quo. Even people who want their spose to overcome an addiction to alcohol may themselves be enablers in the addiction.

This unreliability of support from others in our ventures into new territory, forces us back to our own mind, or rather double mind. We care about what others think—and we should! Even those who say—usually with vehemence—that they do not care what others think, really do. It would bother them immensely, for example, if they thought that others thought that they cared what others think! In protesting too loudly, they reveal that their apparent defiance is but the other side of the same coin of dependency. They are concerned about their image in the eyes of others. But caring about what others think and being dependent upon what others think are two different things. If you are to take responsibility for your own life under God, your primary concern is not what others think but the strength of your own determination.

All thoughts about change challenge the present moment. This is why you are most likely to act when you get fed up with things as they are now. Some thoughts of change are also a judgment on your past. The older we get, the more past we accumulate. Some of us need to protect this past—otherwise a major portion of our life will come under judgment. While conducting a workshop for pastors on pastoral counseling, I stressed the need people have for confession. One older pastor resisted me continuously, stating that confession should be made to God and not to people. I arranged to talk with him privately in order to discuss his concerns more deeply. It was not long before his voice began to quaver and tears came to his eyes. "In all forty years of my ministry," he said, "I could count on one hand the number of people who have come to me for counsel." Then I understood his resistance. The emphasis on confession was placing a negative judgment on his life's work.

Thoughts of change may also seem to be a judgment on our past and present models. Many of us have had persons in our lives who have been influential in our development. Consciously or unconsciously we may seek to emulate them in one way or another. The desire for change may mean a change also of models; but this is really no judgment on our previous models. Life is a process, a movement, in which things rarely stay the same, particularly if we are growing. One who served as a model in the past need not necessarily be the model for the present. Yet our misgivings over making this change may not be the only obstacle to the transition. The models themselves may take it hard. Freud, for example, inspired many followers. Some of these—like Adler, Jung, Rank—after a time developed theories that differed from those of the master. Rather than rejoicing that his followers were taking off on their own, Freud was offended and attacked them, as well as their positions. In the same way, parents, teachers, and other leaders may feel rejected when those who formerly followed their principles begin developing in different ways. Yet, when models become fixed in a rigidly defended status quo, they become idols who must be defended rather than evaluated.

Internal Block to Movement

Since there are so many environmental obstacles in the way of change, we can see how important our own role is in making these changes. Yet our own role contains its own obstacle, namely, our double-mindedness. Double-mindedness is an internal block to movement; it sees to it that desires for change come to nothing. In this sense, our double-mindedness is itself a protection against taking risks. When the double mind is hidden in our subconscious, it is more likely to be victorious in its sabotage of movement than when we are aware of it, since that which is hidden has the advantage of a wider latitude of operation. It often hides behind disguises; for example, if I say, "I can't," there seems to be little that I or anyone else can quarrel with. If I can't, I can't. But as Fritz Perls has pointed out, "I can't" may really mean "I won't." "I won't" sounds defiant, and in saying so I may provoke a conflict, but "I can't" simply sounds helpless. Yet behind the defiant "I won't" may hide the whimpering "I'm afraid to," which may be even less acceptable than "I won't." "I can't" implies that I am innocent and therefore, not responsible. But "I won't" takes on responsibility and invites judgment. "I'm frightened" exposes our vulnerability—our double-mindedness—and may cause embarrassment.

Although Saint Paul says "I can't" in Romans 7, he agonizes over it. "For I do not do what I want, but I do the very thing I hate." But why should he do what he hates? "Now if I do what I do not want . . . it is no longer I that do it, but sin which dwells within me." Sin then is the saboteur. But is it not he, Paul, who is doing the sinning? We see this same obliqueness toward the double mind in his conclusion. "For I delight in the law of God, in my inmost self, but I see in my members another law at war with the law of my mind and making me captive to the law of sin which dwells in my members." To be sure, the frustration we experience in our defeats is evidence of our helplessness—of our captivity to alien forces. Yet, those forces—"sin," the "other law at war in our mind"—are also my forces. I am helpless—my frustration is indicative of this—but I am also culpable. This is why I feel guilty as well as frustrated. For if I do not do what I want, it is because I also do not want to do it. Only as I bring this unpleasant reality into the open can I begin to deal realistically with my problem. I am double-minded.

When I ask a student in academic difficulty whether he or she believes it is possible to do the work sufficient to pass a test or write a paper, and the reply is, "I have to," or, "I must," or, "I have no choice," I have learned to anticipate failure. In fact, I will probably say, "Since you put it that way, I don't think you'll do it." This of course, is disconcerting, and so I explain, "When you say, 'I have to,' you are trying to convince yourself that you have no other options. Then you do not have to fear yourself. The die is cast. But the fact is that you can sabotage your efforts even though you know it means failure. And you are more likely to do so when you believe external pressures will prevent it."

Theologically speaking, what I am describing to such students is the impotency of the "law" in producing change. When I say, "You have to," or, "You have no choice," to others, I simply invite resistance within them. The same thing happens when I say these words to myself. When I say, "I have to," I am in effect saying that I have no choice. But I do. And since I am not facing my other option—the hidden double mind—it is more likely to win out. On the other hand, when a student says, "I know it will be tough, but I intend to do it," or, "I will do it," I am more encouraged. The affirmation "I will" places the responsibility on myself and not on external pressures, and therefore, is more likely to be predictive. Also, "I will" implies that I have affirmed myself in the face of alternative choices, thus showing a more realistic assessment of my inner complexity.

A different kind of double-mindedness is revealed in the assertion, "This is the way I am—this is me!" Obviously, little change can take place in the face of such defiant support of the status quo. This is actually a pseudo-self-affirmation—the counterpart of the self-putdown—and equally as successful in sabotaging movement. Both "This is the way I am" and "I never do anything right" serve as protection against the risks involved in making changes I am frightened about. When I say, "This is the way I am," the implication is, "This is the way I should be," or "am destined to be," and therefore, "the way I intend to remain." Change then becomes an attack on my identity.

This defense against change is an unanticipated consequence of our emphasis in recent times on "liking me" and "affirming me." The implication is that if I like me, I obviously would not want to change me. Liking me, therefore, means "staying the way I am." Liking in this instance implies approving rather than accepting. Since there is supposedly nothing unlikable about me, why shouldn't I like me! This is actually a single-mindedness about myself, but one based on denial. The result is a pseudo-acceptance that is used to support my own inertia. "I'm OK" is distorted to mean "I'm OK the way I am, and if you don't like it, that's just too bad!"

In contrast, a genuine acceptance is based on forgiveness. In forgiveness, the negative about me has obviously been openly faced. In receiving forgiveness, I am obligated to make whatever changes or reparations I can regarding my negative attitudes and behavior. I do not live just to or for myself. Others rightly have expectations of me, including God. The same God who accepts me as I am through forgiveness also calls me to grow, to change, to be a responsible person, to live as his child. Similarly, because I accept others as they are, I care enough about them to confront them if I am concerned about their attitudes or behavior. This is called "tough love," a term associated with chemical addiction treatment centers where such confrontation based on acceptance is necessary to jolt people into recognizing the reality of their addiction. Love as acceptance without expectations is indulgence, and like the "cheap grace" it reflects, is ultimately destructive. Yet, confrontation without love as acceptance is really an attack based on rejection and is, if anything even more destructive.

To resist the idea of change because it supposedly reflects a criticism of the way I am is really just a new version of the old tendency to hold fast to the status quo. "I am the way I am" is the same as saying, "Let's keep things the way they are." What I am used to, I am familiar with, and therefore, feel safer with— even when I am referring to the way I function. Change threatens to upset whatever balance I have achieved, opening me up to all sorts of imagined hornet's nests. Jesus probably had this tendency in mind when he said, "No one after drinking old wine desires new; for he says, 'The old is good' " (Luke 5:39). Actually the old wine is good because it is aged. But in this instance, the relative merit of old and new wine is not the factor that predisposes the choice of the old; rather, it is human inertia, in which having already tasted the old, we see no reason to risk what we already have in choosing the new. So new horizons, goals, and challenges are sacrificed to maintaining the comfort zone of our protected niche.

You may believe that as with old wine, what you are accustomed to is actually better than what might come through change, and you may be right. You may, however, wish to talk this over with someone who has a more objective view of things, to test out whether you may be defending yourself against change. You may also be holding to the status quo because you do not believe you could accept the possible negative consequences implicit in the risks that change entails. If this is the case, you are to be commended for saying so, rather than hiding this reason behind a facade of more objective evaluations. I would think, however, that you will want to grow in your inner security so that you can on occasion accept the risks of change for whatever expansion such change may provide in your development as a person.

There is a similar double-mindedness about change among those with problems of addiction. Most of us hate to admit we are helpless in our addictions, and so we cultivate the delusional mind-set that we can quit anytime we want to. However, the fact is that we cannot afford to test out this delusion, because our desire for whatever it is we are addicted to has become a compulsion before which no desire to quit has a chance unless it receives mighty reinforcement. Our powerlessness over our addiction is the result of a previous abrogation of power. There was a time when we could have exercised the power of choice, but that is long gone after we have consistently sided with the addiction until our entire way of functioning has become dependent upon it. So to break the addiction we need help to restore this power. The program of Alcoholics Anonymous offers the social and spriritual support needed for this restoration in the case of alcoholism and is used also for other forms of addiction. In this program, tough love is used to break through the delusional defenses we in our double-mindedness erect against facing our responsibilities.

Becoming Responsible in Our Decisions

When we are responsible, we choose our own responses to stimuli rather than reacting as conditioned by the addiction. In one sense, we are all addicts in that we are conditioned to react to certain situations as we have so often in the past. We play the old tapes in stimulus-reaction predictability as though we were following a script. It seems we have lost the freedom to do otherwise. Like any addict, we are probably double-minded about choosing a different response, since we are receiving at least some satisfaction from the reaction that is so easily predicted. Finally we may get fed up with the old tapes because we see how counterproductive they are for our other desires and goals. But by now the conditioning is heavily entrenched, and in spite of our better intentions, we may react in the same old way in famil-

iar situations. What often happens, then, is that we get discouraged. In losing our courage, we cease to persist in our efforts and
instead despairingly accept our impotence. "Wretched man that
I am! Who will deliver me from this body of death?" (Rom.
7:24). Who has not at some time or another felt this same despair? What can restore to us the courage to "hang in there"?

Here is where faith comes to our rescue. Becoming discouraged over our own impotency need not be the end of the road; in
fact it can initiate our looking elsewhere for power. Losing confidence in our own power, we can turn to the Higher Power.
When all your own efforts end in frustration, you can still cry to
God for help. "Help" is the simplest of prayers. Directed to
Another, it points beyond our own resources—it is the beginning of trust. No longer dependent upon our own resources, we
can face up to the double-mindedness that has crippled what
little power we had. Our power is restored when we trust in the
Power beyond our own.

This restored power shows itself initially as you make a decision, a commitment, in regard to your double-mindedness. You
choose which of your minds you will identify with. So where
does this leave you? To whom or what are you committed? Insight is one thing, acting on the insight is another. Things will
begin to change in your life when you leave the role of observer
and become a participant. Single-mindedness—your single-
mindedness—begins in commitment—your commitment. This
provides the framework within which you view the issues with
which you struggle. It is the rationale that helps you make your
decisions. I am not referring now to carrying out your commitment but to deciding to whom or what you want to belong, to
cleave, to adhere. Of course you are double-minded about this,
but if you had to make a choice, where would you come down?
Your trust in the Higher Power makes such a decision more
likely since you are not then alone in your decision. Your faith
not only gives you the assurance of God's help, but also provides
a sense of direction—his direction.

As an illustration of how this happens, I will use one of my own addictions. For years I had used an inhaler during the night to clear my clogged nostrils. I told myself I would not get back to sleep if I did not use it. I would have to use it; otherwise, I would become anxious over not getting enough breath. In discussing this with a physician, I was bluntly informed that I was addicted to the inhaler. Although I initially resisted the idea, I soon realized that my sense of security at night was in feeling the inhaler in my pajama pocket as I retired. I also became more aware of the desperation I experienced when I could not find the inhaler prior to retiring. I would keep looking until I did find it.

Convinced I was addicted, I decided I did not want to be. Quitting cold turkey sent me into a state of anxiety, and so I began my "withdrawal" in my daily devotional meditation. As a response to God's calling, I visualized myself able to breathe without the inhaler and sent this mental picture to God as a prayer. Nothing happened for a couple of years. Only in meditation did I have the power. Then I developed the most severe head cold I have ever experienced. Nothing opened my nostrils—not even the inhaler. Accepting the fact that the inhaler was useless, I actually went to sleep breathing through my mouth. That was it! I have never used the inhaler since.

Did the meditative visualization do it? Obviously not, if one understands such meditating purely as mental conditioning. The answer is yes, however, if one understands such meditation also as prayer. The "deliverance" took an event that I certainly did not plan but that God obviously used.

So, one acts in faith in whatever way is open to one in the present moment. The trouble is we usually want instant results. It is hard to wait—to trust. Our responsibility is to set ourselves in the right direction. The results are beyond our responsibility. Let them be where they belong—in our vision of faith. Then wait—"wait for the Lord" (Ps. 27:14).

8

The Good Side of
Double-Mindedness

It is time now to deal with the fact that single-mindedness in itself is no virtue. Persons who affirm their uniqueness in a way that dismisses any need for change, as discussed in the previous chapter, are an illustration of this fact. The determination to escape from responsibility, run from reality, or act out the feelings of the moment is usually based on the desire for instant and simple answers to complex questions and problems.

When I was a college chaplain, I never felt more helpless than when I tried to encourage unhappy freshmen to stick out their first year when they wanted to leave. Nothing—no argument, appeal, or challenge—was ever seriously considered, because their desire—single-mindedness—to leave was so overwhelming. As a parish pastor, I experienced this same kind of helplessness in counseling with persons who wanted out of their marriages because they had discovered a more satisfying relationship with someone else. All my efforts to encourage them to give their marriage another chance—to really work on it—were met by a single-minded desire to end it. The new relationship, although only several months old and untested by responsibility, made the continuance of the marriage, representing an investment of years, sometimes decades, of their life, unthinkable.

Destructive Single-Mindedness

The word ruthless describes a specific kind of destructive single-mindedness, namely, the determination to get to where one wants to go even if it means stepping on others to get there. Ruthless people know what they want and go for it unencumbered by the usual restraints of conscience and compassion. Evidently either they never consider the destructiveness of their single-mindedness or they rationalize away all opposing values.

The colonization by whites of lands inhabited by people of other races is a sad illustration from history of such ruthlessness. Because the whites held to so-called Christian values, they had to find a way to rationalize their genocidal approach to people whose lands they coveted. Almost always this was accomplished by denying that the dark-skinned natives were really human or by asserting that their humanity was so inferior that they really could not be treated as people. So American Indians were "savages." Therefore they could be deceived, robbed, and murdered in good conscience. In Africa the blacks were "uncivilized." So trickery and slaughter were justified in bringing to them the "benefits of civilization." After one such slaughter of black warriors armed only with spears by a British contingent armed with machine guns, a British soldier wrote in his diary that the "pluck" of those warriors would have done credit even to a "civilized" brigade like his own. Nor is this rationalized ruthlessness confined to previous centuries. In a case recently brought to light in one of our northern cities, a policeman allegedly shot and killed a young black man after a chase over a broken taillight and justified both the killing and a subsequent cover-up by saying, "After all, he's nothing but a goddamned nigger kid."

The cultural mind-set that values one group of people over another and justifies crimes against the "inferior" group on this basis, is known as fascism in our modern era. The holocaust by the Nazis against Jews, Gypsies, and the handicapped on the basis of Aryan supremacy is the most flagrant example. When persons as individuals rather than as members of a group show this same lack of compassion in their crimes against others, they are frequently labeled sociopathic, which means literally, "socially sick." Such persons feel no regret for the most heinous of crimes. In their own defense, they show a similar kind of reasoning: their victims "ask for it" or "deserve it." In my own community "queer bashers" beat a man to death because he was a homosexual. One of the killers spoke for this mind-set: "The faggot got what he deserved!"

For all practical purposes, addicts are destructively single-minded, whether chemically addicted or otherwise. Addicts need what it is they are addicted to so badly that they "down" the opposing mind. The double-mindedness over their addiction, therefore, is deeply repressed, if not stilled altogether. The fact that a crisis may restore it again to consciousness indicates that the potential for the double mind probably remains in what seems to be a single-minded desire.

For a model of negative single-mindedness, Kierkegaard suggests the devil. The devil, he says, is sheer spirit. By this he means that the devil is totally conscious and totally integrated. He has no conflicts about what he is doing nor is there any subliminal resistance. His is an unmitigated, unqualified opposition to God. Yet in terms of ultimate accomplishment, he is a total failure, since his destination is the "lake of fire," when the "kingdoms of this world become Christ's."

A similar negative integration is revealed in Shakespeare's words for King Richard III, "Evil, be thou my good." The demonic devastators of the earth, typified, perhaps unfairly, by Richard III, are so thoroughly distorted that they believe evil to be good. The world has suffered immeasurably from their single-minded distortion. Jesus warned against committing the sin against the Holy Spirit, which, he said, was unforgivable because no repentance (change of mind) was possible for those who went to this degree of distorted integration. To commit the sin against the Holy Spirit then, would mean that one had so single-mindedly pursued evil as one's good that one had no conflict—double-mindedness—that would permit one to change.

The incident that precipitated Jesus' warning was one in which good was called evil. In his ministry to the people, he had healed a person who was possessed by a demon so that he could not speak. The people who witnessed the healing marveled at what had happened, but the Pharisees disparaged it by saying, "It is only by Beelzebul, the prince of demons, that this man casts out demons." Jesus countered by saying, "If it is by the Spirit of God that I cast out demons, then the kingdom of God has come upon you" (Matt. 12:24,28). These Pharisees were so set in their determination to be negative toward Jesus that they called a miracle of healing an evil act.

Simplistic Single-Mindedness

Not all destructive single-mindedness is necessarily ruthless or demonic. Some is characterized more by rigidity and inflexibility. Human life is a dynamic process. Though we may resist change in our own lives, it will surely take place in our surroundings. Since things are constantly changing, we humans need constantly to adapt to these changing conditions. If we do not, we become "dated" in our responses. Because of such datedness, some of us may be single-mindedly "out of sync" with our surroundings.

This datedness of response is a familiar obstacle encountered in counseling. People respond to changing conditions as they did before the conditions had changed and thereby create a lot of unnecessary conflict. Because of the single-mindedness of their response, however, they do not see their own role in these conflicts. Ed grew up in a large family where he soon discovered that if he did not aggressively take what he wanted, he got nothing. Some of his most painful memories concern his laments to his parents that his siblings were taking unfair advantage of him, their response to which was to shame him for being a "crybaby." So he learned to keep his feelings to himself as he went on the offensive as the only way to defend himself in the family jungle. The problem began when he left home and continued to react in the same aggressive way in new surroundings where his "survival" was no longer the issue. Although his wife was fascinated by his "macho" strength, she became increasingly aware that she really did not know him. Nor for that matter did anyone else. He was a good man in any team sport because he was an aggressive competitor against all opponents. Yet as he grew older, there was less and less need for these qualities and more and more need for the sensitivity he had long repressed.

What brought Ed to counseling was a family crisis. His children had to depend on their mother for their emotional needs, and she in turn found the burden too much to bear because of her own emotional deprivation in the marriage. She became depressed, and Ed reacted in the only way he knew—first with verbal scorn for weakness and then with appeals to will power. Obviously, he only made matters worse.

Counseling with Ed meant helping him to see that his way of responding once made sense. Perhaps it was his only way of survival in the family in which he grew up. But now that which once was a realistic way of adapting had become destructive. Ed never realized that he had "left home"—that his wife was not his mother and his children were not his siblings, and because of this, his "new" home was in shambles. When he began to see that he could be sensitive and vulnerable in his new home and nothing terrible would happen to him, the long-submerged tender side of Ed began to be exposed, and he became what his "new" family needed.

Like Ed, some of us become the way we are in order to "survive." Later, we continue to see all problems as survival problems and under this pressure react habitually in dated ways—only to make matters worse. For others of us, survival has meant resisting pressure from other people in order to preserve our own identity. It probably made sense to persist in our own way when we originally adopted this reaction, but now it may only make us stubborn and bullheaded. Just once, we ought to break the pattern and give in—negotiate—change our ways—in order to see that nothing catastrophic happens to us because we abandon a dated single-mindedness.

In my counseling there are times, ironically, when I wish some people had more rather than less conflict about their behavior. I long for a bit of double-mindedness that I might tap for their ultimate growth and healing. People, for instance, who should feel guilty over their insensitive and destructive ways may instead reveal a single-minded feeling of "rightness" about them. In my earlier days I would press for guilt—raising questions about their behavior that might stimulate their conscience—only to meet increased resistance to any such consideration. When I abandoned this approach and simply listened to their stories, I discovered more often than not that after half an hour or so these same people would be less vehement about their rightness and perhaps even indicate some doubt about it. If I followed up the doubt, I often found myself listening to a confession.

Mary was like this. She was adamant in our first visit that Joe, her husband, was impossible to live with and that she was justified in leaving him. When, in my impatience, I asked her if she were aware of any contribution she might have made to their problem, she quickly answered, "Yes—I've put up with him too long. I should have made this move years ago!" Learning the hard way once again, I accepted her where she was. It was really no surprise when in her second visit she dropped an aside that I just barely heard: "I probably haven't been the easiest person to get along with either."

"How do you mean?" I asked.

"Oh, well, I say things I suppose I shouldn't—particularly when I'm mad."

"Could you give me an example?" I asked.

"Hm—oh, like yesterday. I sort of blew up when he was late again for supper. Then I found out that he really couldn't help it since he had run out of gas."

"How is it that he couldn't help it?"

"Of course, he could have checked the gauge—but I had run it low the night before, and I forgot to tell him."

What actually happens in instances like this is that people expect to be criticized for their position, and so they put up their defenses. When, however, such criticism does not come, they may lower their defenses and become more open. Their need to be honest may come to the fore and, like Mary, they may become more able to face the double-mindedness that lay dormant behind their impassioned, unyielding rightness. Once the doubt is faced, the conflict within breaks the hold of this destructive single-mindedness.

Ignoring Other Considerations

Destructive single-mindedness depends on blocking out considerations that constitute what it means to be human. The ruthless must block out compassion; ethical considerations have to be rationalized away. The stubborn and simplistic are insensitive to the needs of others; the welfare of the community has to be identified with my welfare. The single-minded who must win at all costs often lie and cheat and sometimes maim and kill to achieve their ends.

While such single-minded pursuit may accomplish a great deal—often building "empires" of one sort or another—the question has to be raised, Is it worth it? Is it worth the ravaging of values that make for human dignity and integrity and that enhance life-in-community? Institutions usually come into being to meet human needs, but tend to stay in being to meet their own needs. This change is rationalized by saying that what is good for the institution—the oil company, the union, the university, the hospital, the church on the corner—is good for the community, whereas the community may actually be being "ripped off."

Yet this same community may support these institutions even as they undermine it. Because of this destructive connivance between institutions and the people they supposedly serve, a judge refused to give a heavy sentence to a coach who was convicted of twenty-one counts of fraud and making false public vouchers in his building of a winning team. "The question is, how fair is it to incarcerate in prison a man for doing what almost everyone in the community wanted him to do—namely, win basketball games.[12] With this justification, Judge Phillip Baiamonte proceeded to give the lightest possible sentence to University of New Mexico basketball coach Norm Ellenberger. So widespread is this community encouragement to win at all costs that Jim Dutcher, basketball coach of the University of Minnesota, responded to the Baiamonte comment by saying, "There is plenty of evidence that if you're fired for cheating, you can get another job. If you're fired for not winning enough, you better find another profession."[13] It is this sort of community-institution cooperation in distorted single-mindedness that moved *Sojourners* editor Danny Collum to say, "Christians must find a way to turn this country away from a social order whose gods are economic growth, national security, and private profit and toward one which recognizes God's image in each person."[14]

The single-minded pursuit of business profits further illustrates how the public health can be sacrificed to institutional interests. In a part of Canada that includes an Indian reservation, a paper mill dumped its waste, containing mercury, into the local lake. The reason?—it was the most economical way to do it. This same lake provided the livelihood for the Indians of the reservation, who were commercial fishermen. But as the mercury input increased, the fish in the lake became too contaminated for human consumption, and the Indian economy was ruined. Forced onto welfare, their independence destroyed, many of the Indians became victims of chemical dependency. The simplistic priority of business profits together with a racism that devalues Indians account for this sad story. Decisions that destroy the environment leave a woeful legacy to future generations, since they chart a course that ultimately will be destructive to all life on this planet.

Double-Mindedness Due to Empathy

While those with simplistic single-mindedness can often make decisions quickly and thus give the impression of being strong persons, their quick decisions are frequently wrongheaded since their supposed strength is actually a weakness. Naturally, it is easier to make decisions if we screen out considerations of such factors as compassion, ethics, and concern for the environment, but such simplifying is really falsifying, since the data that remain are imbalanced and incomplete. It would be much better to postpone such decisions in favor of struggling with them in their recognized and legitimate complexity. The various factors in this complexity are frequently in conflict—hence the desire to disregard some of them—but we need to work through the conflict with as much caring and wisdom as we can muster. When we come to a decision after much struggling and soul-searching, we tend to be modest about our rightness, since we are all too aware of the complexity of the issues. Such modesty is not a sign of weakness but rather of a sober realization of this complexity.

Decisions, as we have discussed previously, are inevitable, regardless of how we go about arriving at them. Some of us tend to postpone making decisions in the hope that they will be made for us in the course of events, so we need not feel responsible if they turn out to be wrong decisions. Procrastinating until we "discover" that deadlines are past is one example. The struggling process in that case is not to reach a decision but to substitute for deciding. We play the game of "look-how-hard-I'm-working-at-it" in lieu of doing it.

Since decisions, whether directly or indirectly made, are inevitable, we need to make our decisions consciously out of strength rather than letting them be made for us due to our indecisiveness. If we believe that a decision has been made for us or that we have been "forced" to make it because of external pressures, we usually do not cooperate well with it. We may even resist its implementation, though outwardly we appear to go along with it. So it is important for our involvement to make our decisions actively rather than passively and to accept the pain of struggle that some decisions require. The "gray areas" make a decision "tough" but not impossible. The complex web of issues involved in decisions that affect other people shows that we should not attempt to make this kind of decision in isolation. Talking the issues over with the others affected—as well as with disinterested counselors—is an important part of the search for wisdom. As we utilize as many resources as are available to us, we need to remind ourselves that our purpose is to arrive at a decision and not simply to prolong the process.

Regardless of the decision that is ultimately made, we need to believe that we have made it. Though others may be involved—and often are—in the decision making process, the result of the process needs to be a consensus. Otherwise we—or others—will "drag our feet" in following through on it. This is particularly the case when the issue of authority is involved. Since those in positions of authority seem to have more weight in decision-making, they may get more passive than active cooperation from those under their authority. The power struggles that frequently characterize conflicts in the parent-child relationship are an obvious illustration.

Thomas Gordon has devised his Parent Effectiveness Training as a way of resolving these otherwise "no-win" situations. In areas of conflict, parents can assert their authority by deciding the issue: "I'm your parent. I'm making the decision. That's it!" This would be Plan A. The child is likely to resist either actively or passively. The parent, however, may "capitulate" to the child: "All right, go ahead. You drive me up the wall!" This would be Plan B. In this instance, the parents are likely to blame the child for any problems that result, thus disclaiming responsibility for the decision. A third option is to go through the difficult chore of "talking it out"—parent and child—in an effort to arrive at Plan C, which would be a consensus decision. Not *my* way or *your* way, but *our* way. Since both parties own responsibility for the decision, each is likely to work toward seeing that it "works."

One of the big reasons some of us shy away from taking responsibility for decisions is that the decision could turn out to be the wrong decision. We are overly concerned about "covering our posterior"—protecting our vulnerability. This is a defensive way of living—like settling for the "lowest common denominator." A student shared with me what a close friend once told him, namely, that he was "made to be vulnerable." At first he was confused by the remark and then angered. Later, he saw more clearly what she meant and felt good about it. Because he was not a defensive person, he often, in his openness, risked himself—that is, risked making mistakes. This meant that he was sometimes hurt—but it also meant that he was close to people and had warm, caring relationships. You—and I—have this same option. It is freeing to take it—to be unburdened of our defensiveness—and to take the leap of faith in trust.

Since avoiding decisions is a delusional escape from reality, what we need instead is support for making them. This, I believe, comes from our faith in God. If we have to be certain that our decision is correct before we make it, obviously we can never—consciously at least—make it. But if we believe that there is One who is bigger than our mistakes and blunders, we may have the courage to go ahead. Although we make them with "fear and trembling," knowing full well our limitations, we can also make them with confidence, believing that God is able to "pick up the pieces" should we be wrong. He is not bound by our limits.

Double-mindedness that is not faced or that is permitted to sabotage our supposed affirmations is one thing; double-mindedness due to the complexity of the issue, to the struggle of an honest and realistic assessment, to the difficult job of facing and sorting out, is entirely another. The former readily results in a defensive single-mindedness familiarly described as, "My mind's made up—don't confuse me with the facts." When this is our attitude, we resist any enlargement of the problem—including additional data—because we need to keep things simplistic so we can feel good about our chosen course. We curtain off the area so we can handle it. However, the kind of double-mindedness that allows the curtain to be removed so that new data can complicate things results in a single-mindedness that is usually accompanied by a "leap in faith."

Questionable Assumptions of Single-Mindedness

In every option for change there are some things we have to give up. To decide for change, then, means that we are willing to give them up. It is important, therefore, to face up to what these "benefits" are that go with our old ways; otherwise their hold on us will persist behind the cover of darkness. This is more likely to occur when there are pressures on us from outside ourselves to change. Opting for change under these conditions frequently results in a single-mindedness that contains the seeds of its own dissolution. The immediate pressure clouds or even temporarily dispels our resistance. Suppose, however, the advantages of change pointed out by others fail to materialize—or that they do materialize but our appreciation of them diminishes. Then the old "benefits" are most likley to come seductively to mind, and we may question whether the "sacrifice" of them was justified.

This is a potential problem in many marital reconciliations.

When a marriage is threatening to dissolve, one of the partners—usually the ostensibly guilty one—may promise almost anything in an effort to persuade the other partner to accept a reconciliation. How genuine are such decisions for change? What happens to them when the crisis has passed?

This is what bothered Nan. During her fifteen years of marriage to Jim, she had lost most of her confidence. One day she decided to move out before she lost it all. Because he was insensitive to her feelings, Jim was not aware of how desperate Nan was. When she left him, he realized how much he wanted and needed her. In his desperation, he went to a counselor and seemed genuine in his repentance. Even Nan was impressed. One day they came to the counselor together. "He seems changed," she said, "I know he's trying hard. But how do I know he is sincere—that he isn't just trying to get me back—and that if I do return it will last?"

The counselor turned to Jim. "I guess the ball is in your court," he said. Jim winced. "I can understand how she feels," he said, "and we have talked about this. All I can say is—I don't like the way I was any more than she does. I want this marriage very much—in fact more than anything else I know. But I'll tell you this—I want to change. And even if we don't get back together—I still want to change."

"How are you going to get your ego boost if you don't have someone to put down?" asked the counselor. Once again Jim winced. "I've thought about this too. I believe I'll get all the ego boost I'll need from being a different kind of person. Remember, I didn't like me then either." The counselor looked to Nan. She was near tears. Yet she too has a responsibility for the reconciliation. Can she give Jim the support—the encouragement—he needs as he struggles to become the person he seems genuinely to want to be? As one changed husband put it, "The more I consider the good she sees in me, the more I try to be like that." And as Charlie Shedd says in his *Letters to Karen,* "You can only tell him he isn't wonderful when he isn't, if you have told him he is wonderful when he is."[15]

Another area where crisis-oriented single-mindedness is a potential problem is in illness. If you are sick—in pain, disabled—why would you not want to get well? Yet it is a question that all of us should raise when we are ill. Jesus asked this question of the paralytic as he was lined up for healing by the pool of Bethesda. Why would he be there if he did not desire to be healed? Yet he had no one with him to place his paralyzed body into the water when the inner springs began bubbling. According to the legend the first one in at that moment would be healed. He was there but he also was not there. So the question is, "Do you want to be healed?"

In our illnesses, we may not come to the bubbling waters without the wherewithal to get in, but we may show the same double-mindedness toward healing. We say, "It's in the physician's hands." In spite of all the necessary things that physicians do to bring healing, healing does not lie in the physician's hands. Yet we continue to hold to the belief that it does, probably because it allows us to avoid our own responsibility for healing.

If we take the question seriously—Do you want to get well?—we should explore the possible "benefits" that come from being sick. We have previously discussed one of the more common benefits, namely, the need for suffering to control our level of guilt. Suffering is a form of punishment, and sickness may provide it. The benefit in sickness thus is that it protects us from even greater suffering, the dread of which is stimulated by our low self-esteem.

Another benefit in illness is that it legitimates a dependent lifestyle. Of all the excuses that we put forth to explain our inadequacy, none is more foolproof than illness. It is assumed that because of your pain or other indispositions, you are excused. "I'm not feeling well enough to do it," will have to give way to doing it, should healing come.

A third benefit is closely related to the above. The role we have in the family may be shaped by our illness. In addition to being legitimately excused from responsibilities other members of the family have, our illness brings with it special attention that may be hard to give up. "How are you feeling?" the others ask apprehensively. There is usually little mutuality in this concern, for in our illnesses we rarely have enough empathy to inquire about the other's health. If illness makes us "something special," we may resist becoming like everyone else by getting well.

We could add to these common benefits all of the unique advantages that come to this or that person through illness. Obviously, the concept of the passive patient is a myth. The will to healing when one is ill is not unlike the will to live when one is faced with death. We recognize the latter as a powerful influence for life, while the former is rarely taken seriously because of the assumption of single-mindedness regarding healing.

In our desire to leave our old ways, we need to ask ourselves what we are being excused from—justified in or protected from—in these old ways. If these questions are not dealt with seriously, our efforts to change will be undercut by a desire for these old advantages. Our unacknowledged double-mindedness is behind some of our relapses. So open your eyes and face your choices. Give yourself the freedom not to change. What are the advantages in either course? The disadvantages? How now to decide?—the question takes us back to our identity again. Who is the person that you want to be? Who is the person you feel good about—and with? This question posits the larger context within which tough decisions are made and tough affirmations are given. Religiously speaking, the question is one of calling. As creatures we do not live only to ourselves. Our response to the question of identity is really a response to the God who created us.

Called to Enter the New

In the description of double-mindedness and its consequences, I have used words and images that related to the story
of the Exodus. Double-mindedness, as we have seen, can immo-
bilize us with inner conflict so that we go in circles rather than in
any one direction. We need to deal with this double-mindedness
so that we can leave these old and unprofitable ways to which we
have been captive and enter into new ventures in freedom. In
this concluding chapter I will focus on the climax to which these
images have been pointing—the entry into the new, "the promised land."

Two Pivotal Events in the Exodus

There are two pivotal events in the story of the Exodus, one at
the beginning and the other at the end. When the Hebrew people fled the land of Egypt where they had been enslaved, they
were pursued by the Egyptian army. Although the Egyptian
pharaoh had agreed to let them go after the firstborn of Egyptian families died during the night of the Passover, he changed
his mind once they had left. When the people under the leadership of Moses reached the Red Sea, they saw coming behind
them the Egyptian soldiers. They were trapped. It was then that
Moses in prayer to God raised his arms toward the sea. According to the story, winds then parted the sea and the fleeing slaves
crossed over on dry land. When the Egyptians tried to follow

them, the winds ceased, the water returned, and they were drowned.

The other event, to which I referred in a previous chapter, took place as they were nearing the land of Canaan that God had promised to them as the place they could live in freedom. Although this promised land was the goal of all of their journeying, the closer they came to it the more apprehensive these people became. The majority report of the spies spoke to and for the fears of the people. "We can't go in there," these spies said. "Everybody in the land is a giant and we are as grasshoppers in their eyes and in our own." Isn't this the way it seems when we are frightened? Everybody else is a giant and we see ourselves as grasshoppers beside them.

The two spies who gave the minority report said, in effect, "They are not all giants and we surely are not grasshoppers. The same God who delivered us at the Red Sea and has accompanied us in our journey with mighty signs will go with us. So let us continue to trust Him and enter!" But the people were too frightened to hear them. One of these spies was their future leader Joshua. When he persisted, the people finally threatened to silence him by killing him. Their single-minded pursuit of freedom was undermined by fear; they refusd to enter. So they wandered in the wilderness for the rest of their lives.

The first of these events of the Exodus shows God's power to deliver. The second shows the decisive nature of human resistance to that power. Perhaps the people were not so different at the beginning than they were at the end. At the Red Sea they had no room to retreat or to mark time. Though frightened, they could not turn back. Unfortunately, at the other end they *could* turn back when frightened—and did.

Wandering in the Wilderness

The wanderings in the wilderness reflect a pattern of futility that was not of God's doing. As the Letter to the Hebrews says,

"They were unable to enter because of unbelief" (Heb. 3:19). Theirs was a lack of faith, of vision. This remarkable epistle in the New Testament portrays the Exodus not only as the primal story of Hebrew history, but also as a parable of what can happen to every person. In this parable, the promised land is called God's rest, since this is the word that Psalm 95, which the writer is quoting, uses to describe the promised land. God's rest marks a place or time of completion, of fulfillment, of peace. "Therefore, while the promise of entering his rest remains, let us fear lest any of you be judged to have failed to reach it" (Heb. 4:1).

Fear, as we have seen, is not a destructive attitude or passion so long as we fear the right thing. For the writer of the Letter to the Hebrews, the truly dreadful object for fear is to fail to enter into God's rest. This is more than the tragedy of unfulfilled potential; it is the tragedy of living one's life going in circles. This is the lament of the laments—that some of us "chicken out" in our moments of opportunity and spend our lives wandering aimlessly in barren circles. Obviously, it becomes a personal challenge to keep this from happening not only to ourselves but also to others. So the appeal, "Exhort one another every day, as long as it is called 'today'" (Heb. 3:13). Who knows how much an encouraging or even confronting word from a caring person at a critical moment will influence whether one enters or wanders. For good or ill, social support—or pressure—has a lot to do with the choices we make. So let us use it for good! When you sense your aloneness and need reinforcement, you can reach out for it. Make contact—even if only by phone—with someone whom you know to be understanding and (after inquiring whether he or she has a moment to talk) share where you are and ask for feedback. "As long as it is called today." As long as you do it *today* there is hope. If you postpone it to some indefinite tomorrow, that hope may pass.

As long as it is called today we can also act to change our situation. It is not unusual for people to get bogged down in cyclic futility, in which rather than newness of life, there is only discouragement. As the word indicates, when we are *dis*couraged, we lack the courage to act—to enter whatever new possibilities are present. Yet we may feel quite the opposite, namely, that we lack a challenge—that we are stuck in a rut.

The focus of this discouragement is frequently one's job. According to our cultural anticipations, a job is supposed to do something for us. It is a way we get, or at least prove, our worth. Even if we do not believe that we get our worth through our job—including the job we do as a spouse or parent—it is still difficult in our culture not to be influenced by this pressure. Whether one is a salesperson, a pastor, a teacher, a secretary, a foreman, a custodian, or a full-time homemaker, one is counting on the job to provide some purpose and meaning to one's life. Students have a similar anticipation from college. Should our anticipations not be realized, we tend to get "fed up" with school, tired of the job, or disillusioned with the profession.

One of the major factors we look for in a job is its potential for advancement. Upward mobility is very important for satisfaction in what we are doing. For parenthood this means that our children do well. We all need a challenge and upward mobility or promotion seems to be what provides it in our culture. If we get stuck somewhere along the line, we tend to become dispirited and wish for a change.

My observation is that double-mindedness plays its role in these job ruts. There are usually also reasons for staying where we are—special advantages we may lose if we change jobs, people we feel obligated to, the salary we are getting, the need to finish what we have begun. It all adds up to the complexity that, as we have noted, tends to characterize difficult decisions. There are also risks in making a move, even in initiating the process. Because of our double-mindedness we may find it less threatening to stay where we are, but we do so disgruntledly. I know of a woman who turned down the job she had been trying for years to get. When I asked her why, she said she could not work out the transitional arrangements that she desired.

Although our ruts have plenty of justification in our surroundings, they are primarily a state of mind. Some situations are intolerable and we should act to change them. Others are intolerable to us, but for reasons other than the situation itself. Although barely thirty, Fred had a job that most people in his field of engineering would have desired. But he hated it. "I know I should be happy where I am, but I'm not," he said. "Something's missing and it's affecting my whole life." It turned out that what was missing was something a job could not give him. But in our culturally conditioned thinking, it is the most likely place to put the blame. Fred was missing something within himself; his defense system consisted in keeping himself hidden behind a facade of charm so that he was lacking the satisfaction of close relationships. He needed help to improve his relationships, including his relationship with himself, so that he could receive more from his job.

It is not God's doing if we become stuck in our old ways. We can enter the new, or as the Letter to the Hebrews says, "We who have believed enter that rest" (Heb. 4:3). We often associate entering into God's rest with the time of death. Rest in Peace is spoken at gravesides and engraved on tombstones. Eternal rest is a synonym for life in heaven or for whatever else we may describe as our final destiny as God's people. In using the Exodus as a parable of every person's odyssey, the ultimate meaning of the promised land is eternal life. Yet eternal life is something we receive now as well as anticipate after death. As Saint Paul describes it, "Now I know in part; then I shall understand fully, even as I have been fully understood" (1 Cor. 13:12). What we shall receive in heaven is connected with what we can receive now as a foretaste. Because of this connection, the present moment is in reality the "eternal now."

For the Letter to the Hebrews, entering into rest is a present potential. "Today, when you hear his voice, do not harden your hearts" (Heb. 3:15). Our entry is in response to hearing God's voice—his call to us to come. The new is now—if we can accept it. Quoting the prophet Isaiah, Saint Paul affirms the immediacy of the opportunity. "Behold, now is the acceptable time" (2 Cor. 6:2). There is a now-ness to the newness.

Yet in spite of this possibility of entering into the new—our "rest," the "promised land"—in any present moment, we instead tend to get mired in the repetition of wandering, going in circles, destined by double-mindedness to a cyclic existence. To make matters even more ironic, we are—as we have seen— enablers to our wanderings, conspirators in our cyclic existence.

Although our bogged-down-ness may be ironic in the face of such moment by moment opportunities, it is not beyond understanding. It is frightening to enter any new situation, state of being, or approach to life. We can get just as "chicken-hearted" as the Hebrews when their fears over entering the promised land enlarged their opponents in that land into invincible giants. Fear, as we have noted, is a basic cause of double-mindedness. Some of us have disturbing dreams when we are involved in any new situation. Not all of the anxiety over the new is addressed consciously, and so the subconscious unloads its share into our dreams. Interestingly enough, it is not unusual for some people also to have disturbing dreams when they are experiencing no external stress. In fact, they may be experiencing a plateau of calm, but since it is not their usual way of living, the pull back to a previous more stressful existence is experienced in dreams. The reservoir of anxiety in the subconscious in this way restores the balance of stress to its more usual level.

One may also have less internal stress when faced with troubles shared by the community. This is because we project our internal stress onto the community concern. After Mount Saint Helens erupted and sent volcanic ash all over the area, for example, mental health centers noted a twenty-five percent drop in clients. Although the eruption was frightening, residents also found in it a common excitement that monopolized their attention and energy—a truly integrating experience.

Some trace the fear of entering into a new venture to the birth trauma. Traumatized by the violent experience of being born, according to the theory, we tend to seek our rest by withdrawal—ultimately, to the safety of our mother's womb and even to the fetal position, which some mentally ill patients assume as their fixed position. In withdrawing, we are reversing the direction of growth and maturation because the traumatic introduction to maturation has afflicted us with terror at every possible renewal of it.

The pioneer in this interpretation of human withdrawal is psychoanalyst Otto Rank, whose treatise on this subject attributes almost every neurotic and psychotic reaction to this early psychic wound. Since Rank, practitioners have developed a rebirthing process, basically a therapy of suggestion through which people are taken back in their history to "recall" the traumas of their birth. They then "go through" the process mentally once more, only this time as a positive experience. English theologian and psychologist Frank Lake is a foremost practitioner of this art. Lake taught at my seminary as one of the replacements for me while I was on a sabbatical and led several of our students in the rebirthing process. They valued it highly, although I myself have never had this experience.

Paralleling this rebirthing process is the natural childbirth movement pionered by Dr. Frank LeBoyer. We would not need this rebirthing, says LeBoyer, if we did a better job in the birthing process. The trauma of a baby's birth can be reduced by providing a quiet and dark atmosphere with warmth and tender touch into which the baby can emerge—an environment not unlike the womb that it is leaving. Although I am a layperson in these matters, the attempt to reduce the birth trauma makes sense to me. I have been appalled by some of the birthing procedures of the medical establishment that we have experienced as a family.

Regardless of the origins of our immobilizing fears at the entrance to new experiences, we obviously find it tempting to go with our regressing mind and to withdraw in these times of stress. Sometimes this is necessary to give us the time and space to reflect and center ourselves. Periods of personal growth from childhood to adulthood may be preceded by periods of apparent regression. We may need to feel and act like a baby again when the challenge of growth seems too much. It is to be hoped that we will get the parenting we need at these times to be able to return to the challenge and accept it.

But as the Letter to the Hebrews solemnly warns, one can permanently retreat and wander in the wilderness of regression for the remainder of one's life, immobilized in spirit as rigidly as is the body of a catatonic. I mentioned the birth trauma to illustrate the complexity of our temptation to withdraw at these times. Though our birth is not something we remember, we are influenced in our development by events in our life that have occured prior to memory or that we otherwise do not recall. While it may be helpful—God can work through this as well as in other ways—I do not believe it is necessary to be rebirthed or to undergo any other type of recall therapy in order to gain the courage to enter into the new. I believe, as I trust has been evidenced, that we have the resources in our faith in Christ to provide us with this courage.

Dying of the Old, Rising of the New

Before the Hebrews finally entered the promised land, the older generation had died. As an old man, Joshua was able to inspire the new generation to make the effort. In this respect also the story is every person's story. The dying of the old and the rising of the new is the familiar New Testament description of how we grow in our Christian identity. The above description, however, is based on the New Testament story of the death and resurrection of Christ. As Christ died on the cross for the sins of the world we who believe in him die with him to our sinful nature, and as his resurrection is his victory over death and all of its dark symbols, so we rise with him to "newness of life." Even the death of our bodies is viewed in a similarly productive way. Referring to our inevitable demise Saint Paul says, "What you sow does not come to life unless it dies. . . . What is sown is perishable, what is raised is imperishable. . . . It [our body] is sown in weakness, it is raised in power" (1 Cor. 15:36, 42, 43). The seed must "die" before the plant can come forth. But while we still live in this body, our spirit undergoes a figurative death and resurrection again and again as the way of growth. We die repeatedly, often in the throes of crises, to our old, dated, and destructive ways and rise to new and creative ways.

But the process is not automatic. The calling and power is of God, but we also are involved. What then is our role? The Letter to the Hebrews is clear: "Strive to enter that rest, that no one fall by the same sort of disobedience [as the older generation of Hebrews]" (Heb. 4:11). Strive to enter! This is a directive that Americans particularly can understand. "Strive to enter" is ominously similar to the familiar appeals to willpower and hard work that have helped to fulfill the American dream. Actually, striving in this context is not an appeal to effort in the usual sense. Entrance into rest does not come from hard work or willpower. Striving here means something other than taking the initiative or acting aggressively. In fact, it may appear to some to be more passive than active. In contrast to that of the American production system, in the context of faith the initiative belongs to God. He is calling us to enter. Our "effort" therefore is one of response—of believing his promise to go with us, of trusting him even when in our discouragement and disappointment, he seems hidden or absent.

Those who see passivity in the "activities" of believing or of trusting fail to perceive what the opposite of these activities would be. Again, the story of the Exodus clearly protrays these. The people panicked rather than trusted; they resisted the call to enter rather than follow it. They could have listened to Joshua rather than to their fears. We humans are never inactive until we are dead. We are always moving in one direction or another, and though our double-mindedness about this direction may bring us outwardly to a halt, our inward behavior continues in the agitation of fear and frustration.

Although the English spelling would not so indicate, the name Joshua is really the same as Jesus in Hebrew and means "Yahweh is salvation." The meaning of this salvation goes beyond the deliverance of the Hebrews from their slavery in Egypt to their freedom in the promised land. As the Letter to the Hebrews says, "If Joshua had given them rest, God would not speak later of another day." This other day is "today, when you hear his voice" (Heb. 4:8, 7). The rest to which we are now called is mediated by Jesus and has its meaning in eternal life, which is available to us now in part and fully in eternity.

Striving to enter may actually mean *ceasing* what we are doing. So much of our activity is counterproductive to our so-called goals because of the sabotaging influence of our double-mindedness. Striving to enter means, for example, ceasing our resistance to change. It means giving up the "payoffs" of familiarity, because we see how illusory is its security. Our immediate reaction to even the thought of such "ceasing" is fear. What will happen! While we may be nebulous about what it is we fear, it is really death. We see death in any threatening situation; each is a symptom of death or a symbol of it. These symbols resemble the nightmarish giants that lie in wait to attack us in a new venture or the nightmarish panics over becoming lost in a strange place.

The fear that stopped the ancient Hebrews can also stop us. The antidote to fear is also the same as theirs, namely, trusting in God, who calls us to enter. Like death, any new venture—

promised land, rest—is without our accustomed signposts. It is territory into which "we walk by faith, not by sight" (2 Cor. 5:7). We can talk with the pioneers, and this helps a great deal. But although they encourage us to strive to enter, they cannot enter for us.

For the ultimate venture of faith, namely, entering into our own death, who are the pioneers? What about the people whom Raymond Moody wrote about in *Life After Life* who had been clinically dead and then revived? Haven't they been there? The answer for me is a dialectical one. What appears to be a state of death could still be a state of life. On the other hand the "experience" of death has changed these people. Like Moody's cases, those with whom I have talked who have had this experience do not fear death as they once did. In this sense they have "been there."

It is the fear of death—with all of its symbols—that causes us to hold on to the old rather than to let go so that we can take God's "hand" as he bids us enter. Yet, ironically, it is holding on to the old and resisting entering the new that leads to death. Our tenacity—or perversity—in holding to that which is destructive as a way of avoiding destruction indicates how much we are governed by illusion. Eric Berne expressed this irony from the therapist's viewpoint when he said, "It is harder to give up failure than success."

Perhaps the best explanation for our propensity for illusion is the way our imagination fortifies our fears. The Hebrews really believed that all of their opponents were giants and that they themselves were as grasshoppers. The fact that such was not true was simply beyond their comprehension. Our imagination fixes us to our fears by embellishing them with images too horrendous for rational rebuttal. One is literally locked into illusion by the unlimited capacity of the imagination to reinforce one's fears. Imagination itself is not the problem, however, since it is simply the capacity of the human mind to image, to envision, to "see" pictures. Yet imagination is a powerful faculty for good or ill, depending on what is stimulating it. The same imagination that binds us to illusion when it is hooked up to our fears can free us to risk entering the new when hooked up to our faith. When we listen to God's voice as he calls us through Jesus to enter into his rest, our imagination envisioning this rest is an incentive to enter.

The longer we hold to old ways the more they seem to be right. Habituation, it appears, leads to legitimization. This is part of the illusional system that blinds us to truth. We may need "permission," therefore, to leave the old and enter the new. We need an authoritative OK. Berne is right in his use of these terms, but where does the OK come from? As Christians we receive it from Jesus, who leads us into the promised rest. Six times in the Sermon on the Mount he encourages his followers to leave the old and embrace the new. "You have heard that it was said to the men of old . . . but I say to you." For example, "You have heard that it was said, 'An eye for an eye and a tooth for a tooth,' But I say to you, Do not resist one who is evil. But if any one strikes you on the right cheek, turn to him the other also" (Matt. 5:21, 38-39).

We are not bound to past voices, our own or others—even other authorities and old models, what was "said to the men of old." "Therefore, if any one is in Christ, he is a new creation; the old has passed away, behold, the new has come" (2 Cor. 5:17). These words describe the dynamic nature of the Christian calling—always changing, growing, risking, entering. Having received permission from Jesus, "the pioneer and perfector of our faith" (Heb. 12:2), we need now to let go of old ways to which we have become habituated, rather than hold on to them as though they perpetuated our security. We need to let go not only for our own sake but also for others. We do not live in isolation; rather, in ways small or large, we influence others even as we are influenced by them. We "let go" also for our

friends, our children, our spouse, our parents, and anyone else
for whom we may, however minimally, serve as models. At the
times when I find myself most under pressure to react in old and
bankrupt ways, I remind myself that it is not just me that this
concerns but also my children, and that if I can listen to God's
voice and follow him into new and better ways, I can more
single-mindedly pray for them in their own encounters with
similar trials.

Ultimately, of course, we "let go" for God, in faithfulness to
our commitment. God does more than give us permission to
enter the new, he also calls us. The idea of permission implies
that we are allowed to enter. God's call offers more than this. He
cares about our responses; he wants us to enter—a mere permis-
sion-giver might remain indifferent. The difference is reflected
in the enigmatic introduction to the Ten Commandments. 'I the
Lord your God am a jealous God" (Exod. 20:5). The word
jealous in this context is not our usual pejorative describing one
who, in his or her insecurity, needs to possess another exclusive-
ly. Rather, this description of God as jealous means he is the
opposite of indifferent. He cares about us and what we do. The
promised rest to which he calls us is his gift. He jealously—
passionately—wants us to receive it. He is, as Francis Thomp-
son said, "the hound of heaven," who persists in his overtures of
"everlasting love" (Jer. 31:3). Life with—and under—God
consists in our receiving continuously this "newness" of life that
he desires us to have.

The Inner Shrine

Life is still stressful though we enter into rest. The world
continues to be a "fallen" world and we, as well as the people
with whom we live and work, continue to be "fallen" people.
The new that we enter is still within the old social order where
greed is more evident than compassion. Though the quality of
life continues to change, we are still subject to reverses, disap-

pointments, regressions, and inexplicable tragedies. Just recently, my wife and I talked with a young couple whose child was killed when she was hit by a car driven by an intoxicated driver. They were deeply hurt by so needless a tragedy, and their grief was coupled with rage. "I honestly don't think I'm angry with God," the father said, "I believe he is troubled also by what has happened. But I am angry at a society that permits intoxicated people to drive cars that kill wonderful people like my daughter!" We knew what he meant because several years ago we experienced a similar loss. The protest comes from deep within one's devastated soul: "Why—why do such things happen?"

What then is different about our life as we enter his rest? What happens to us is one thing—how we interpret it is another. People are fond of saying, "Time heals." Actually time in itself heals nothing; in fact it may make matters worse. I have seen people who with time became increasingly bitter and withdrawn following a tragic or otherwise disappointing event. It takes time to heal, but it takes more than time. It also takes faith and trust. The key factor is how we interpret what we perceive with our senses. How we interpret the events that take place in our lives determines how we feel about them. This in turn shapes and develops our motives and intentions, which then influence our behavior—our actions. If our interpretation is fuzzy, distorted, or confused, the resulting double-mindedness will jumble our intentions and inhibit our actions.

It is precisely in this critically important area of interpretation that entering into God's rest makes its impact. The context of the *new*—in which our identity as creatures under God is the dominant characteristic—provides a vantage point for "getting our head together." In this milieu of trust, there is a distinct and renewable perspective within which to "fit things"—to "make up our mind."

Although the *new* is a state of being, it is also figuratively a place. Here the analogy of the promised land continues. The "place" of rest is like an inner shrine that we can enter for renewal of perspective and assurance. It is the vortex of the whirlpool, the still spot in the center of the whirlwind. Here we can retreat in the midst of our involvements in order to clarify our interpretations. Here we become once again aware of God's presence—an awareness we may lose when away from the shrine. In the commitment of faith we cease to be immobile before the double-mindedness due to fear and guilt; instead the hope implicit in faith indicates the direction in which to move. At the shrine our imagination takes the leap of faith to picture its fulfillment. With this vision before us, we can endure. Our energies, seemingly depleted by stress from without and dissipating conflict within, are again restored.

The obstacle to entering the new is that, as creatures of habit, we are bound to stimulus-reaction patterns that perpetuate the old. How to break out of this bondage? Being conditioned to old ways, how can we become unconditioned?—or even better, conditioned to new ways? Imaging can help us move in this direction. In a previous chapter I told how I worked on my addiction to an inhaler by imaging in a prayerful mind-set my breathing freely without the inhaler. I even visualized myself throwing the inhaler away because I did not need it. Similarly, one can see oneself responding differently to old stimuli. Choosing one's response in this way is like the rebirthing process described previously. One can visualize one's bondage to stimulus-reaction and say no to it and then visualize choosing a different response. Imaging within the inner shrine thus pioneers our entering into the new. We are simultaneously praying these mental pictures. When we use words in prayer we are simply using auditory symbols for these mental pictures. Here we are using only the pictures, which God can receive just as well.

I myself begin this process by imaging the double mind, because I believe I also want to follow the old conditioning. Then I

direct myself to choose between my minds—to make the choice
to enter the new. Next I "hear" God's call to me to come in this
direction. I "see" myself turning off the old tapes and moving
toward God. I anticipate the impulses and compulsions and
habitual reactions that will threaten to reverse my course, and
mentally cancel them. Then I envision myself with courage entering the new.

We not only live in a fallen world, we are also fallen persons.
We not only can, but do, regress. Biblically put, "The desires of
the flesh [our propensity for destructive ways] are against the
Spirit [God's dwelling within us], and the desires of the Spirit
are against the flesh; for these are opposed to each other, to
prevent you from doing what you would" (Gal. 5:17). Dealing
with double-mindedness means also learning to live with it.
Saint Paul's familiar lament, "For I do not do the good I want,
but the evil I do not want is what I do" (Rom. 7:19)—despite its
exclusion of complicity—is one that we shall continue to identify with. From the perspective of rest even our regressions, however, are not a total loss. God can use what he does not will.
Through his influence on us, these regressions are converted
into dyings to the old and entries into the new. Regressions,
within this interpretation, reveal to us new data—wisdom—
about ourselves that are helpful to our growth. God may withdraw his gift (rest) so that he can more fully give it. To say this is
obviously a human way of referring to God. Yet what other ways
have we to talk about God than human ways! The truth is that
we need to endure the dips to experience the rises, to "die" in
order to gain the insight needed for further growth. As we have
seen, our guilt (over regressions), when we are forgiven, is a
stimulus for change, since it provides us with our own feedback
on our behavior that enlarges not only our self-understanding,
but also the influence upon us of our relationship with God (the
Spirit). I find it helpful to keep a journal in which to write the
insights into myself and others that come through these regres-

sions. I also include the insights that come through my "victories." One can learn from both, when one sees them in the light of God's care and call.

The rest into which we enter again and again is a source of constant renewal. It is a "place"—a temple of the Spirit of God within—where we can give our full attention to his presence and receive the reassurance that "our times are in his hand" (Ps. 31:15, paraphrase). In this inner sanctuary we can renew our trust as well as our commitment. The counterpart of this shrine within is the House of God—the sanctuary, the church—where the presence of God that fills heaven and earth is localized in the symbols of an edifice. Although church sanctuaries differ in the nature of their structure, they are usually characterized by stimuli to worship through pictures, other visual symbols, architectural design, and furnishings.

These buildings, however, despite their tangible symbols, are incomplete as sanctuaries without the community—the people of God, the fellowship of believers—that congregates there to worship. We need each other as members of the corporate body, as ministers one to another. Even as the symbols of the sanctuary are stimuli to sight, so the symbols used by the worshipping body stimulate also our hearing. The music, the singing of the service, and the liturgy involve us in a more totally sensorial way in the rest that centers in worship.

These stimuli to sight and hearing of the people of God gathered in the House of God correspond in the inner shrine to a similar stimulation produced by our imaginative capacity to see and hear. The inner sanctuary with its mental visualization needs the outer sanctuary to maintain its identity, even as the outer sanctuary with its tangible identity needs the inner sanctuary for its integrity. We need the place, the House of God, and the tangible support, the fellowship of believers, to assist our entries into rest where we know that He, and none of his creatures, including ourselves, is God. In this rest there is resonance between creature and Creator that leads to creative single-mindedness, in which power and energy are received and restored for good doing. The single-mindedness that ensues is creative, because it is shaped by our response to the calling of God, in whose image we are created, and therefore is a response from our own identity.

We have come to the end of exploring the debilitating effects of double-mindedness and, by contrast, the creative release that comes when we make up our minds. You may feel like the man who said to me, "I know I need to make up my mind, and I'm trying—but it is such a struggle!"

"Who are you struggling with?" I asked.

He paused a bit and then said, with a vulnerable smile, "Myself, I suppose."

"If you are struggling with yourself," I said, "you obviously have some control over the struggle."

There are many factors in our lives over which we have little if any control. But in areas where I struggle with me, I have something to do with bringing closure to the struggle.

So cut through the fog of protective confusion and hear the call of God—which is there for the listening. You are not alone in your struggle, because your destiny is in that call. God wants you to get off dead center and move with his creative process. Making up your mind, then, is really responding to the call of your Creator to follow your destiny as one created in his image. Making the move to enter into the new is creative single-mindedness.

Notes

1. Carl A. Whitaker and Augustus V. Napier, *The Family Crucible* (New York: Harper & Row, 1978), p. 276.
2. O. Carl Simonton, Stephanie Mathews-Simonton, James Creighton, *Getting Well Again* (New York: St. Martin's Press, 1978), pp. 74-75.
3. Virginia Satir, *People Making* (Palo Alto, Calif.: Science & Behavior Books, 1972), p. 250.
4. Albert Ellis, *How to Live With or Without Anger* (New York: Reader's Digest Press, 1977), p. 76.
5. Kathryn Koob, *Lutheran Standard,* May 15, 1981, p. 9.
6. Ben Patterson, Editorial, *Wittenburg Door,* December/January 1981, p. 4.
7. Phyllis McGinley, "Garland of Precepts," *The Love Letters of Phyllis McGinley* (New York: Viking, 1954), p. 7.
8. Daniel Yankelovich, "New Rules in American Life: Searching for Self-Fulfillment in a World Turned Upside Down," *Psychology Today,* April 1981, p. 40.
9. Ibid.
10. Toni Morrison, *Song of Solomon* (New York: Signet, 1978), p. 75.
11. Norman Cousins, "Cousins Says Heal Thyself," *Minneapolis Star,* May 27, 1981.
12. *St. Paul Dispatch,* July 26, 1981.
13. Ibid.
14. Danny Collum, "Assault on the Poor," *Sojourners,* July 1981, p. 16.
15. Charlie Shedd, *Letters to Karen: On Keeping Love in Marriage* (New York: Avon Books, 1968), p. 44.